SPECIAL NEEDS IN ORDINARY SCHOOLS
General Editor: Peter Mittler

Developing Mathematical and Scientific Thinking in Young Children

Special Needs in Ordinary Schools

General editor: Peter Mittler
Associate editors: James Hogg, Peter Pumfrey, Tessa Roberts, Colin Robson
Honorary advisory board: Neville Bennett, Marion Blythman, George Cooke, John Fish, Ken Jones, Sylvia Phillips, Klaus Wedell, Phillip Williams

Titles in this series

Developing Mathematical and Scientific Thinking in Young Children

David Womack

Cassell

This book is dedicated . . .

To those children I have known—who struggled to know

Cassell Educational Limited
Artillery House
Artillery Row
London SW1P 1RT

First published 1988

British Library Cataloguing in Publication Data

Womack, David
  Developing mathematical and scientific
  thinking in young children.—(Special
  needs in ordinary schools)
  1. Primary schools. Curriculum subjects:
  Science—For teaching
  I. Title   II. Series
  372.3'5

ISBN: 0–304–31397–1

Phototypesetting by Fakenham Photosetting Ltd
Printed and bound in Great Britain by Mackays of Chatham PLC, Chatham, Kent

Contents

Foreword: Towards education for all

AIMS

This series aims to support teachers as they respond to the challenge they face in meeting the needs of all children in their school, particularly those identified as having special educational needs.

Although there have been many useful publications in the field of special educational needs during the last decade, the distinguishing feature of the present series of volumes lies in their concern with specific areas of the curriculum in primary and secondary schools. We have tried to produce a series of conceptually coherent and professionally relevant books, each of which is concerned with ways in which children with varying levels of ability and motivation can be taught together. The books draw on the experience of practising teachers, teacher trainers and researchers and seek to provide practical guidelines on ways in which specific areas of the curriculum can be made more accessible to all children. The volumes provide many examples of curriculum adaptation, classroom activities, teacher–child interactions, as well as the mobilisation of resources inside and outside the school.

The series is organised largely in terms of age and subject groupings, but three 'overview' volumes have been prepared in order to provide an account of some major current issues and developments. Seamus Hegarty's *Meeting Special Needs in Ordinary Schools* gives an introduction to the field of special needs as a whole, whilst Sheila Wolfendale's *Primary Schools and Special Needs* and John Sayer's *Secondary Schools for All?* address issues more specifically concerned with primary and secondary schools respectively. We hope that curriculum specialists will find essential background and contextual material in these overview volumes.

In addition, a section of this series will be concerned with examples of obstacles to learning. All of these specific special needs can be seen on a continuum ranging from mild to severe, or from temporary and transient to long-standing or permanent. These include difficulties in learning or in adjustment and behaviour, as well as problems resulting largely from sensory or physical impairments or from difficulties of communication from whatever cause. We hope that teachers will consult the volumes in this section for guidance on working with children with specific difficulties.

The series aims to make a modest 'distance learning' contribution to meeting the needs of teachers working with the whole range of pupils with special educational needs by offering a set of resource materials relating to specific areas of the primary and secondary curriculum and by suggesting ways in which learning obstacles, whatever their origin, can be identified and addressed.

We hope that these materials will not only be used for private study but be subjected to critical scrutiny by school-based inservice groups sharing common curricular interests and by staff of institutions of higher education concerned with both special needs teaching and specific curriculum areas. The series has been planned to provide a resource for Local Education Authority (LEA) advisers, specialist teachers from all sectors of the education service, educational psychologists, and teacher working parties. We hope that the books will provide a stimulus for dialogue and serve as catalysts for improved practice.

It is our hope that parents will also be encouraged to read about new ideas in teaching children with special needs so that they can be in a better position to work in partnership with teachers on the basis of an informed and critical understanding of current difficulties and developments. The goal of 'Education for All' can only be reached if we succeed in developing a working partnership between teachers, pupils, parents, and the community at large.

ELEMENTS OF A WHOLE-SCHOOL APPROACH

Meeting special educational needs in ordinary schools is much more than a process of opening school doors to admit children previously placed in special schools. It involves a radical re-examination of what all schools have to offer all children. Our efforts will be judged in the long term by our success with children who are already in ordinary schools but whose needs are not being met, for whatever reason.

The additional challenge of achieving full educational as well as social integration for children now in special schools needs to be seen in the wider context of a major reappraisal of what ordinary schools have to offer the pupils already in them. The debate about integration of handicapped and disabled children in ordinary schools should not be allowed to overshadow the movement for curriculum reform in the schools themselves. If successful, this could promote the fuller integration of the children already in the schools.

If this is the aim of current policy, as it is of this series of unit-texts, we have to begin by examining ways in which schools and school policies can themselves be a major element in children's difficulties.

Can schools cause special needs?

Traditionally, we have looked for causes of learning difficulty in the child. Children have been subjected to tests and investigations by doctors, psychologists and teachers with the aim of pinpointing the nature of the problem and in the hope that this might lead to specific programmes of teaching and intervention. We less frequently ask ourselves whether what and how we teach and the way in which we organise and manage our schools could themselves be a major cause of children's difficulties.

The shift of emphasis towards a whole-school policy is sometimes described in terms of a move away from the deficit or medical model of special education towards a more environmental or ecological model. Clearly, we are concerned here with an interaction between the two. No one would deny that the origins of some learning difficulties do lie in the child. But even where a clear cause can be established—for example, a child with severe brain damage, or one with a serious sensory or motor disorder—it would be simplistic to attribute all the child's learning difficulties to the basic impairment alone.

The ecological model starts from the position that the growth and development of children can be understood only in relation to the nature of their interactions with the various environments which impinge on them and with which they are constantly interacting. These environments include the home and each individual member of the immediate and extended family. Equally important are other children in the neighbourhood and at school, as well as people with whom the child comes into casual or closer contact. We also need to consider the local and wider community and its various institutions—not least, the powerful influence of television, which for some children represents more hours of information intake than is provided by teachers during eleven years of compulsory education. The ecological model thus describes a gradually widening series of concentric circles, each of which provides a powerful series of influences and possibilities for interaction—and therefore learning.

Schools and schooling are only one of many environmental influences affecting the development and learning of children. A great deal has been learned from other environments before the child enters school and much more will be learned after the child leaves full-time education. Schools represent a relatively powerful series of environments, not all concerned with formal learning. During the hours spent in school, it is hard to estimate the extent to which the number and nature of the interactions experienced by any one child are directly concerned with formal teaching and learning. Social interactions with other children also need to be considered.

Questions concerned with access to the curriculum lie at the heart of any whole-school policy. What factors limit the access of certain children to the curriculum? What modifications are necessary to ensure fuller curriculum access? Are there areas of the curriculum from which some children are excluded? Is this because they are thought 'unlikely to be able to benefit'? And even if they are physically present, are there particular lessons or activities which are inaccessible because textbooks or worksheets demand a level of literacy and comprehension which effectively prevent access? Are there tasks in which children partly or wholly fail to understand the language which the teacher is using? Are some teaching styles inappropriate for individual children?

Is it possible that some learning difficulties arise from the ways in which schools are organised and managed? For example, what messages are we conveying when we separate some children from others? How does the language we use to describe certain children reflect our own values and assumptions? How do schools transmit value judgements about children who succeed and those who do not? In the days when there was talk of comprehensive schools being 'grammar schools for all', what hope was there for children who were experiencing significant learning difficulties? And even today, what messages are we transmitting to children and their peers when we exclude them from participation in some school activities? How many children with special needs will be entered for the new General Certificate of Secondary Education (GCSE) examinations? How many have taken or will take part in Technical and Vocational Education Initiative (TVEI) schemes?

The argument here is not that all children should have access to all aspects of the curriculum. Rather it is a plea for the individualisation of learning opportunities for all children. This requires a broad curriculum with a rich choice of learning opportunities designed to suit the very wide range of individual needs.

Curriculum reform

The last decade has seen an increasingly interventionist approach by Her Majesty's Inspectors of Education (HMI), by officials of the

Department of Education and Science (DES) and by individual Secretaries of State. The 'Great Debate', allegedly beginning in 1976, led to a flood of curriculum guidelines from the centre. The garden is secret no longer. Whilst Britain is far from the centrally imposed curriculum found in some other countries, government is increasingly insisting that schools must reflect certain key areas of experience for all pupils, and in particular those concerned with the world of work (*sic*), with science and technology, and with economic awareness. These priorities are also reflected in the prescriptions for teacher education laid down with an increasing degree of firmness from the centre.

There are indications that a major reappraisal of curriculum content and access is already under way and seems to be well supported by teachers. Perhaps the best known and most recent examples can be found in the series of Inner London Education Authority (ILEA) reports concerned with secondary, primary and special education, known as the Hargreaves, Thomas and Fish Reports (ILEA, 1984, 1985a, 1985b). In particular, the Hargreaves Report envisaged a radical reform of the secondary curriculum, based to some extent on his book *Challenge for the Comprehensive School* (Hargreaves, 1982). This envisages a major shift of emphasis from the 'cognitive–academic' curriculum of many secondary schools towards one emphasising more personal involvement by pupils in selecting their own patterns of study from a wider range of choice. If the proposals in these reports were to be even partially implemented, pupils with special needs would stand to benefit from such a wholesale review of the curriculum of the school as a whole.

Pupils with special needs also stand to benefit from other developments in mainstream education. These include new approaches to records of achievement, particularly 'profiling' and a greater emphasis on criterion–referenced assessment. Some caution has already been expressed about the extent to which the new GCSE examinations will reach less able children previously excluded from the Certificate of Secondary Education. Similar caution is justified in relation to the TVEI and the Certificate of Pre-Vocational Education (CPVE). And what about the new training initiatives for school leavers and the 14–19 age group in general? Certainly, the pronouncements of the Manpower Services Commission (MSC) emphasise a policy of provision for all, and have made specific arrangements for young people with special needs, including those with disabilities. In the last analysis, society and its institutions will be judged by their success in preparing the majority of young people to make an effective and valued contribution to the community as a whole.

A CLIMATE OF CHANGE

Despite the very real and sometimes overwhelming difficulties faced by schools and teachers as a result of underfunding and professional unrest, there are encouraging signs of change and reform which, if successful, could have a significant impact not only on children with special needs but on all children. Some of these are briefly mentioned below.

The campaign for equal opportunities

First, we are more aware of the need to confront issues concerned with civil rights and equal opportunities. All professionals concerned with human services are being asked to examine their own attitudes and practices and to question the extent to which these might unwittingly or even deliberately discriminate unfairly against some sections of the population.

We are more conscious than ever of the need to take positive steps to promote the full access of girls and women not only to full educational opportunities but also to the whole range of community resources and services, including employment, leisure, housing, social security and the right to property. We have a similar concern for members of ethnic and religious groups who have been and still are victims of discrimination and restricted opportunities for participation in society and its institutions. It is no accident that the title of the Swann Report on children from ethnic minorities was *Education for All* (Committee of Inquiry, 1985). This too is the theme of the present series and the underlying aim of the movement to meet the whole range of special needs in ordinary schools.

The equal opportunities movement has not itself always fully accepted people with disabilities and special needs. At national level, there is no legislation specifically concerned with discrimination against people with disabilities, though this does exist in some other countries. The Equal Opportunities Commission does not concern itself with disability issues. On the other hand, an increasing number of local authorities and large corporations claim to be 'Equal Opportunities Employers', specifically mentioning disability alongside gender, ethnicity and sexual orientation. Furthermore, the 1986 Disabled Persons Act, arising from a private member's Bill and now on the statute book, seeks to carry forward for adults some of the more positive features of the 1981 Education Act—for example, it provides for the rights of all people with disabilities to take part or be represented in discussion and decision-making concerning services provided for them.

These developments, however, have been largely concerned with children or adults with disabilities, rather than with children already in ordinary schools. Powerful voluntary organisations such as MEN-CAP (the Royal Society for Mentally Handicapped Children and Adults) and the Spastics Society have helped to raise political and public awareness of the needs of children with disabilities and have fought hard and on the whole successfully to secure better services for them and for their families. Similarly, organisations of adults with disabilities, such as the British Council of Organisations for Disabled People, are pressing hard for better quality, integrated education, given their own personal experiences of segregated provision.

Special needs and social disadvantage

Even these developments have largely bypassed two of the largest groups now in special schools: those with moderate learning difficulties and those with emotional and behavioural difficulties. There are no powerful pressure groups to speak for them, for the same reason that no pressure groups speak for the needs of children with special needs already in ordinary schools. Many of these children come from families which do not readily form themselves into associations and pressure groups. Many of their parents are unemployed, on low incomes or dependent on social security; many live in overcrowded conditions in poor quality housing or have long-standing health problems. Some members of these families have themselves experienced school failure and rejection as children.

Problems of poverty and disadvantage are common in families of children with special needs already in ordinary schools. Low achievement and social disadvantage are clearly associated, though it is important not to assume that there is a simple relation between them. Although most children from socially disadvantaged backgrounds have not been identified as low achieving, there is still a high correlation between social-class membership and educational achievement, with middle-class children distancing themselves increasingly in educational achievements and perhaps also socially from children from working-class backgrounds—another form of segregation within what purports to be the mainstream.

The probability of socially disadvantaged children being identified as having special needs is very much greater than in other children. An early estimate suggested that it was more than seven times as high, when social disadvantage was defined by the presence of all three of the following indices: overcrowding (more than 1.5 persons per room), low income (supplementary benefit or free school meals) and adverse family circumstances (coming from a single-parent home or a home with more than five children) (Wedge and Prosser, 1973). Since this study was published, the number of families coming into these categories has greatly increased as a result of deteriorating economic conditions and changing social circumstances.

In this wider sense, the problem of special needs is largely a problem of social disadvantage and poverty. Children with special needs are therefore doubly vulnerable to underestimation of their abilities: first, because of their family and social backgrounds, and second, because of their low achievements. A recent large-scale study of special needs provision in junior schools suggests that while teachers' attitudes to low-achieving children are broadly positive, they are pessimistic about the ability of such children to derive much benefit from increased special needs provision (Croll and Moses, 1985).

Partnership with parents

The Croll and Moses survey of junior school practice confirms that teachers still tend to attribute many children's difficulties to adverse home circumstances. How many times have we heard comments along the lines of 'What can you expect from a child from that kind of family?' Is this not a form of stereotyping at least as damaging as racist and sexist attitudes?

Partnership with parents of socially disadvantaged children thus presents a very different challenge from that portrayed in the many reports of successful practice in some special schools. Nevertheless, the challenge can be and is being met. Paul Widlake's recent books (1984, 1985) give the lie to the oft-expressed view that some parents are 'not interested in their child's education'. Widlake documents project after project in which teachers and parents have worked well together. Many of these projects have involved teachers visiting homes rather than parents attending school meetings. There is also now ample research to show that children whose parents listen to them reading at home tend to read better and to enjoy reading more than other children (Topping and Wolfendale, 1985; see also Sheila Wolfendale's *Primary Schools and Special Needs*, in the present series).

Support in the classroom

If teachers in ordinary schools are to identify and meet the whole range of special needs, including those of children currently in special schools, they are entitled to support. Above all, this must come from the head teacher and from the senior staff of the school; from any special needs specialists or teams already in the school; from members of the new advisory and support services, as well as from educational psychologists, social workers and any health professionals who may be involved.

This support can take many forms. In the past, support meant removing the child for considerable periods of time into the care of remedial teachers either within the school or coming from outside. Withdrawal now tends to be discouraged, partly because it is thought to be another form of segregation within the ordinary school, and therefore in danger of isolating and stigmatising children, and partly because it deprives children of access to lessons and activities available to other children. In a major survey of special needs provision in middle and secondary schools, Clunies-Ross and Wimhurst (1983) showed that children with special needs were most often withdrawn from science and modern languages in order to find the time to give them extra help with literacy.

Many schools and LEAs are exploring ways in which both teachers and children can be supported without withdrawing children from ordinary classes. For example, special needs teachers increasingly are working alongside their colleagues in ordinary classrooms, not just with a small group of children with special needs but also with all children. Others are working as consultants to their colleagues in discussing the level of difficulty demanded of children following a particular course or specific lesson. An account of recent developments in consultancy is given in Hanko (1985), with particular reference to children with difficulties of behaviour or adjustment.

Although traditional remedial education is undergoing radical reform, major problems remain. Implementation of new approaches is uneven both between and within LEAs. Many schools still have a remedial department or are visited by peripatetic remedial teachers who withdraw children for extra tuition in reading with little time for consultation with school staff. Withdrawal is still the preferred mode of providing extra help in primary schools, as suggested in surveys of current practice (Clunies-Ross and Wimhurst, 1983; Hodgson, Clunies-Ross and Hegarty, 1984; Croll and Moses, 1985).

Nevertheless, an increasing number of schools now see withdrawal as only one of a widening range of options, only to be used where the child's individually assessed needs suggest that this is indeed the most appropriate form of provision. Other alternatives are now being considered. The overall aim of most of these involves the development of a working partnership between the ordinary class teacher and members of teams with particular responsibility for meeting special needs. This partnership can take a variety of forms, depending on particular circumstances and individual preferences. Much depends on the sheer credibility of special needs teachers, their perceived capacity to offer support and advice and, where necessary, direct, practical help.

We can think of the presence of the specialist teacher as being on a

continuum of visibility. A 'high-profile' specialist may sit alongside a
pupil with special needs, providing direct assistance and support in
participating in activities being followed by the rest of the class. A
'low-profile' specialist may join with a colleague in what is in effect a
team-teaching situation, perhaps spending a little more time with
individuals or groups with special needs. An even lower profile is
provided by teachers who may not set foot in the classroom at all but
who may spend considerable periods of time in discussion with
colleagues on ways in which the curriculum can be made more
accessible to all the children in the class, including the least able. Such
discussions may involve an examination of textbooks and other reading assignments for readability, conceptual difficulty and relevance
of content, as well as issues concerned with the presentation of the
material, language modes and complexity used to explain what is
required, and the use of different approaches to teacher–pupil dialogue.

IMPLICATIONS FOR TEACHER TRAINING

Issues of training are raised by the authors of the three overview
works in this series but permeate all the volumes concerned with
specific areas of the curriculum or specific areas of special needs.

The scale and complexity of changes taking place in the field of
special needs and the necessary transformation of the teacher-
training curriculum imply an agenda for teacher training that is
nothing less than retraining and supporting every teacher in the
country in working with pupils with special needs.

Although teacher training represented one of the three major
priorities identified by the Warnock Committee, the resources devoted to this priority have been meagre, despite a strong commitment to training from teachers, LEAs, staff of higher education, HMI
and the DES itself. Nevertheless, some positive developments can be
noted (for more detailed accounts of developments in teacher education see Sayer and Jones, 1985 and Robson, Sebba, Mittler and
Davies, 1988).

Initial training

At the initial training level, we now find an insistence that all teachers
in training must be exposed to a compulsory component concerned
with meeting special needs in the ordinary school. The Council for
the Accreditation of Teacher Education (CATE) and HMI seem set to
enforce these criteria; institutions that do not meet them will not be
accredited for teacher training.

Although this policy is welcome from a special needs perspective, many questions remain. Where will the staff to teach these courses come from? What happened to the Warnock recommendations for each teacher-training institution to have a small team of staff specifically concerned with this area? Even when a team exists, they can succeed in 'permeating' a special needs element into initial teacher training only to the extent that they influence all their fellow specialist tutors to widen their teaching perspectives to include children with special needs.

Special needs departments in higher education face similar problems to those confronting special needs teams in secondary schools. They need to gain access to and influence the work of the whole institution. They also need to avoid the situation where the very existence of an active special needs department results in colleagues regarding special needs as someone else's responsibility, not theirs.

Despite these problems, the outlook in the long term is favourable. More and more teachers in training are at least receiving an introduction to special needs; are being encouraged to seek out information on special needs policy and practice in the schools in which they are doing their teaching practice, and are being introduced to a variety of approaches to meeting their needs. Teaching materials are being prepared specifically for initial teacher-training students. Teacher trainers have also been greatly encouraged by the obvious interest and commitment of students to children with special needs; optional and elective courses on this subject have always been over-subscribed.

Inservice courses for designated teachers

Since 1983, the government has funded a series of one-term full-time courses in polytechnics and universities to provide intensive training for designated teachers with specific responsibility for pupils with special needs in ordinary schools (see *Meeting Special Needs in Ordinary Schools* by Seamus Hegarty in this series for information on research on evaluation of their effectiveness). These courses are innovative in a number of respects. They bring LEA and higher-education staff together in a productive working partnership. The seconded teacher, headteacher, LEA adviser and higher-education tutor enter into a commitment to train and support the teachers in becoming change agents in their own schools. Students spend two days a week in their own schools initiating and implementing change. All teachers with designated responsibilities for pupils with special needs have the right to be considered for these one-term courses, which are now a national priority area for which central funding is available. However, not all teachers can gain access to these courses as the institutions are geographically unevenly distributed.

Other inservice courses

The future of inservice education for teachers (INSET) in education in general and special needs in particular is in a state of transition. Since April 1987, the government has abolished the central pooling arrangements which previously funded courses and has replaced these by a system in which LEAs are required to identify their training requirements and to submit these to the DES for funding. LEAs are being asked to negotiate training needs with each school as part of a policy of staff development and appraisal. Special needs is one of nineteen national priority areas that will receive 70 per cent funding from the DES, as is training for further education (FE) staff with special needs responsibilities.

These new arrangements, known as Grant Related Inservice Training (GRIST), will change the face of inservice training for all teachers but time is needed to assess their impact on training opportunities and teacher effectiveness (see Mittler, 1986, for an interim account of the implications of the proposed changes). In the meantime, there is serious concern about the future of secondments for courses longer than one term. Additional staffing will also be needed in higher education to respond to the wider range of demand.

An increasing number of 'teaching packages' have become available for teachers working with pupils with special needs. Some (though not all) of these are well designed and evaluated. Most of them are school-based and can be used by small groups of teachers working under the supervision of a trained tutor.

The best known of these is the Special Needs Action Programme (SNAP) originally developed for Coventry primary schools (Muncey and Ainscow, 1982) but now being adapted for secondary schools. This is based on a form of pyramid training in which coordinators from each school are trained to train colleagues in their own school or sometimes in a consortium of local schools. Evaluation by a National Foundation for Education Research (NFER) research team suggests that SNAP is potentially an effective approach to school-based inservice training, providing that strong management support is guaranteed by the headteacher and by senior LEA staff (see Hegarty, *Meeting Special Needs in Ordinary Schools*, this series, for a brief summary).

Does training work?

Many readers of this series of books are likely to have recent experience of training courses. How many of them led to changes in class-room practice? How often have teachers been frustrated by their inability to introduce and implement change in their schools on returning from a course? How many heads actively support their staff in becoming change agents? How many teachers returning from advanced one-year courses have experienced 'the re-entry phenomenon'? At worst, this is quite simply being ignored: neither the LEA adviser, nor the head nor any one else asks about special interests and skills developed on the course and how these could be most effectively put to good use in the school. Instead, the returning member of staff is put through various re-initiation rituals, ('Enjoyed your holiday?'), or is given responsibilities bearing no relation to interests developed on the course. Not infrequently, colleagues with less experience and fewer qualifications are promoted over their heads during their absence.

At a time of major initiatives in training, it may seem churlish to raise questions about the effectiveness of staff training. It is necessary to do so because training resources are limited and because the morale and motivation of the teaching force depend on satisfaction with what is offered—indeed, on opportunities to negotiate what is available with course providers. Blind faith in training for training's sake soon leads to disillusionment and frustration.

For the last three years, a team of researchers at Manchester University and Huddersfield Polytechnic have been involved in a DES funded project which aimed to assess the impact of a range of inservice courses on teachers working with pupils with special educational needs (see Robson, Sebba, Mittler and Davies, 1988, for a full account and Sebba, 1987, for a briefer interim report). A variety of courses was evaluated; some were held for one evening a week for a term; others were one-week full time; some were award-bearing, others were not. The former included the North-West regional diploma in special needs, the first example of a course developed in total partnership between a university and a polytechnic which allowed students to take modules from either institution and also gave credit recognition to specific Open University and LEA courses. The research also evaluated the effectiveness of an already published and disseminated course on behavioural methods of teaching – the EDY course (Farrell, 1985).

Whether or not the readers of these books are or will be experiencing a training course, or whether their training consists only of the reading of one or more of the books in this series, it may be useful to conclude by highlighting a number of challenges facing teachers and teacher trainers in the coming decades.

1. We are all out of date in relation to the challenges that we face in our work.
2. Training in isolation achieves very little. Training must be seen as part of a wider programme of change and development of the institution as a whole.
3. Each LEA, each school and each agency needs to develop a strategic approach to staff development, involving detailed identification of training and development needs with the staff as a whole and with each individual member of staff.
4. There must be a commitment by management to enable the staff member to try to implement ideas and methods learned on the course.
5. This implies a corresponding commitment by the training institutions to prepare the student to become an agent of change.
6. There is more to training than attending courses. Much can be learned simply by visiting other schools, seeing teachers and other professionals at work in different settings and exchanging ideas and experiences. Many valuable training experiences can be arranged within a single school or agency, or by a group of teachers from different schools meeting regularly to carry out an agreed task.
7. There is now no shortage of books, periodicals, videos and audiovisual aids concerned with the field of special needs. Every school should therefore have a small staff library which can be used as a resource by staff and parents. We hope that the present series of unit texts will make a useful contribution to such a library.

The publishers and I would like to thank the many people—too numerous to mention—who have helped to create this series. In particular we would like to thank the Associate Editors, James Hogg, Peter Pumfrey, Tessa Roberts and Colin Robson, for their active advice and guidance; the Honorary Advisory Board, Neville Bennett, Marion Blythman, George Cooke, John Fish, Ken Jones, Sylvia Phillips, Klaus Wedell and Phillip Williams, for their comments and suggestions; and the teachers, teacher trainers and special needs advisers who took part in our information surveys.

Professor Peter Mittler   University of Manchester
                                                                            January 1987

REFERENCES

Clunies-Ross, L. and Wimhurst, S. (1983) *The Right Balance: Provision for Slow Learners in Secondary Schools*. Windsor: NFER/Nelson.
Committee of Inquiry (1985) *Education for All*. London: HMSO (The Swann Report).
Croll, P. and Moses, D. (1985) *One in Five: The Assessment and Incidence of Special Educational Needs*. London: Routledge & Kegan Paul.
Farrell, P. (ed.); (1985) *EDY: Its Impact on Staff Training in Mental Handicap*. Manchester; Manchester University Press.
Hanko, G. (1985) *Special Needs in Ordinary Classrooms: An Approach to Teacher Support and Pupil Care in Primary and Secondary Schools*. Oxford: Blackwell.
Hargreaves, D. (1982) *Challenge for the Comprehensive School*. London: Routledge & Kegan Paul.
Hodgson, A., Clunies-Ross, L. and Hegarty, S. (1984) *Learning Together*. Windsor: NFER/Nelson.
Inner London Education Authority (1984) *Improving Secondary Education*. London: ILEA (The Hargreaves Report).
Inner London Education Authority (1985a) *Improving Primary Schools*. London: ILEA (The Thomas Report).
Inner London Education Authority (1985b) *Equal Opportunities for All?* London: ILEA (The Fish Report).
Mittler, P. (1986) The new look in inservice training. *British Journal of Special Education*, **13**, 50–51.
Muncey, J. and Ainscow, M. (1982) Launching SNAP in Coventry. *Special Education: Forward Trends*, **10**, 3–5.
Robson, C., Sebba, J., Mittler, P. and Davies, G. (1988) *Inservice Training and Special Needs: Running Short School-Focused Courses*. Manchester: Manchester University Press.
Sayer, J. and Jones, N. (eds) (1985) *Teacher Training and Special Educational Needs*. Beckenham: Croom Helm.
Sebba, J. (1987) The development of short, school-focused INSET courses in special educational needs. *Research Papers in Education* (in press).
Topping, K. and Wolfendale, S. (eds) (1985) *Parental Involvement in Children's Reading*. Beckenham: Croom Helm.
Wedge, P. and Prosser, H. (1973) *Born to Fail?* London: National Children's Bureau.
Widlake, P. (1984) *How to Reach the Hard to Teach*. Milton Keynes: Open University Press.
Widlake, P. (1985) *Reducing Educational Disadvantage*. London: Routledge & Kegan Paul.

Preface

This book is for all who are concerned with the mathematical and scientific development of young children. It is for teachers who are looking for ways to broaden the insights and deepen the understanding of children in their classes who experience difficulty in the learning of either mathematics or science. In particular, the book is aimed at those who have to teach children with special learning needs in ordinary classes and for those who have more general responsibility for the teaching of mathematical and scientific ideas to primary age children.

This is not, however, a book on teaching primary maths and science, nor is it addressed primarily to those teaching in remedial groups or special schools. These subjects and teaching situations have been adequately covered by others and it is assumed here that suitable books on these topics will already be in the hands of those who need them. Indeed, it is likely that teachers reading this book will already be working through some scheme of work in maths and science. Instead, an attempt has been made to include suggestions, ideas and activities that will be helpful to a teacher faced with the challenge of one or more exceptional learners in his or her classroom.

The ability to learn, in common with many other complex human behaviours, forms a continuum of performance—however this performance might be measured. This being so, we would expect to find in any large group of children a wide range of abilities, including those children who by reason of their response to teaching are considered to have learning needs that differ from their peers. Reference has sometimes been made in the past to special groups of children such as 'the more able slow learner' or even 'remedial rabbits' in reception classes. However, the notion of a class of ordinary children containing a 'slow learner' like a goat among sheep is not a useful one. A more realistic picture was painted by the Committee of Enquiry set up in 1974 under the chairmanship of Mary Warnock (the Warnock Report). This stated that as many as one in five children in the ordinary school will have special needs at some time during their school life. In point of fact teachers have always taught children with special needs in their classes and undoubtedly will continue to do so in the future.

But if children have special needs, then so have teachers. My first class as a probationary teacher in the heart of Salford's 'Coronation Street' area contained just such children and because my teaching was not flexible enough to cater for either their interests or their abilities, they caused me many problems. Years later, teaching in a special school, I found the converse problem of attempting to cater for the needs of a bright but hyperactive child whose demands taxed my ingenuity and patience almost to the limit. After a number of years teaching in special schools, I returned to teaching in ordinary schools and found the same children still there, once more testing my resources to the utmost.

Many of the ideas in the central section of this book evolved from these experiences in both ordinary and special schools and also in one-to-one teaching situations with children who for one reason or another were not learning within the conventional framework of state schools. Some activities are set down in the form in which they were used—others have been modified or adapted to provide more flexibility than the particular circumstances in which they were first tried. Some ideas are the common heritage of all maths and science teachers but may never have been presented in a format suitable for use with slower learning children in the classroom. In this sense, then, it is hoped that the book will make more widely available the collective experience of many teachers.

Many of the suggestions are based on the belief that although the *learning* needs of children may differ, there are many topics of common interest to all children. The activities included here are therefore intended to supplement and enrich the teaching of mathematics and science to children of *all* levels of ability. Almost all the ideas are suitable for teaching to groups of any size, including a 'one-to-one' situation, and none requires special materials that are not commonly available both in and out of schools.

Finally, and perhaps most importantly, it is assumed that teachers will wish to teach 'equally' each child in their class, without undue attention to one group of children affecting the quality of education offered to the children in the rest of the class. Such a teaching task is not an easy one. The aim of this book, therefore, is to offer positive help in meeting the needs of both children and teachers in primary maths and science.

I should like to express my gratitude to Colin Robson and Peter Mittler for supporting what I have tried to achieve in this book—and to Anne for always being there.

David Womack   Nairobi, 1988

PART I
Children Learning

I often walk slowly but I never walk backwards
(Handwritten sign hanging on wall of
African student-teacher's college room)

1

Children with special needs

WHO ARE THE CHILDREN AND WHAT ARE THEIR NEEDS?

Since the publication of the Warnock Report (DES, 1978), the distinction between those children requiring a 'special' form of education and those who would be best served by 'ordinary' education is no longer a useful one to make. The Warnock Committee found that as many as one child in five might require special educational help at some stage of school life and this finding reflects the continuum of need and learning development that is found in the ordinary school population.

Probably the largest single category of children who have special needs are those who have been variously described as slow learners, less able children, low attainers or low achievers, etc. However, labels can subtly influence attitudes, despite the intentions of those who use them. Another disadvantage with such labels is their tendency to create mutually exclusive groups, so that a child labelled a slow learner may not at the same time be considered as 'ordinary'. More importantly, labelling can have a profound effect on those who are so labelled, particularly those children with a strong sense of social awareness (Womack, 1983a). Those who have taught children who have been moved at an older age from ordinary schools to special schools will know what a traumatic experience this can be for them since the aspirations and behaviour of children are strongly affected by their classroom peers. Slower learning is not a disease but it *is* catching, and attention should therefore be directed more to the children themselves rather than to any labels we might choose to give them.

If we are no longer to define children by educational category or placement, how can children with special educational needs in the ordinary school be identified and so helped? There are various ways, including staff meetings, observing children at work or play and the discerning use of formal and informal assessments. Such procedures are the concern of another volume in the present series (Wolfendale, 1987).

However, there is much that can be done to facilitate the teaching and learning of less able children in the context of the ordinary school classroom. Specifically, children may have sensory and physical handicaps of a visual, auditory or perceptual–motor nature and these can create problems in the children's understanding of spatial or temporal relationships. Fluctuating attention or hyperactivity can affect an even broader spectrum of learning behaviours and these handicapping symptoms are sometimes treated as the fault of the child, much more so than in the cases of children suffering from more obvious handicaps such as muscular dystrophy, cerebral palsy or spina bifida. Although such physiological handicaps may suggest that little can be done to overcome the resultant learning disabilities, a child's determination and motivation will frequently overcome the most adverse of environmental circumstances. Conversely, environmental factors can also exert a powerful influence on children and evidence from both research and from teachers within the classroom suggests that we should set no limit to the level of attainment we believe any child in our class may reach.

LEARNING AND THE NEED FOR MOTIVATION

Handicapped children do not want to be pitied; neither should they be ignored. If the *causes* of children's learning difficulties are various then so are their *needs*. Needs may initially be social – a longing for acceptance by friends, peers or even the teacher. Teachers may sometimes feel that social problems are not their concern, but much 'social work' can be achieved incidentally in the classroom. For example, a child who is seen to be valued by a teacher will in turn be accorded respect by the rest of the class, and this can have far reaching social benefits.

There are also needs that are even deeper than social needs, and these may be loosely described as 'emotional'. Formal education often attempts to detach learning from the emotional component of the learner's personality and this is particularly marked in the teaching of maths and science. Although there may be good academic reasons for divorcing the affective from the cognitive aspects of understanding, such a separation is not a natural one, for young children or indeed for any adult. Jean Piaget (1969, p. 158) expresses this as follows: 'There is no behaviour pattern, however intellectual, which does not involve affective factors as motives: . . . The two aspects, affective and cognitive are at the same time inseparable and irreducible.'

All children's reactions to life's experiences are inseparably interwoven with affectivity and intentionality. For example, a young child may believe that the scooter from which he has just fallen had the *intention* of hurting him and this is one of the reasons why the scientific concepts of chance and probability are especially difficult for young children to grasp. In a powerfully reasoned book, Margaret Donaldson (1978) has also drawn attention to the difference in quality of children's reasoning in familiar circumstances and their reasoning in contrived experimental or test situations. She suggests that these formal assessment contexts call for 'disembedded thinking', which she defines as 'thought that has been prised out of the old primitive matrix within which originally all our thinking is contained' (p. 76).

Less able children are often characterised by a certain inflexibility in transferring their thoughts rapidly from one situation to another and teachers of such children are usually advised to provide a careful grading of concepts if progress is to be made. However, slower learning children just as frequently need to find a connecting link between concepts at an *affective* level. For example, children's television series that have used stories as the medium for teaching mathematics or English have had much success in capturing and holding the attention of children. The writer's own experience of using such programmes with slower learning children in the classroom suggests that understanding and learning can be greatly enhanced when presented within a motivating context. It seems that once emotional participation in the medium is gained, it sustains an active interest in the learning content. This is a feature of learning for which we have at present no appropriate terminology. However, once initiated, such cognitive involvement creates a *learning momentum* that enables abstract concepts to be held and manipulated at a much more effective level than when motivation is not present.

Motivation, however, needs to be positive. When feelings are confused through apprehension, anxiety or fear, learning may be severely curtailed or may not even take place at all. The powerful adverse effects the emotions can have on ordinary adults learning mathematics have been documented by Laurie Buxton (1981). Such negative experiences, particularly in the early stages of learning, can result in a negative cycle of non-motivation and underachievement and if prolonged may result in a permanent block to learning (see Figure 1.1).

True learning involves a readjustment of existing cognitive structures. For many less able children this involves a considerable effort of will and determination and such perseverance at a learning task requires a high degree of motivation. However, once motivated, a child's involvement and participation will enable cognitive processes to function more freely. Understanding comes with greater involve-

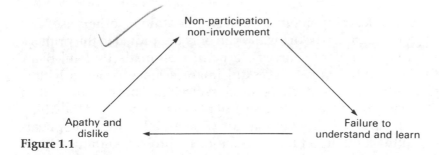

Non-participation,
non-involvement

Apathy and
dislike

Failure to
understand and learn

Figure 1.1

ment at both a cognitive *and* affective level and this involvement increases as the child's interest is captured. The relationship is a circular one of increasingly favourable learning conditions as shown in Figure 1.2. This encapsulates the experience of the writer and

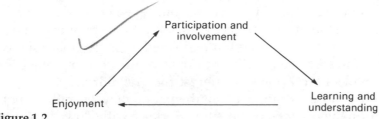

Participation and
involvement

Enjoyment

Learning and
understanding

Figure 1.2

many other teachers that children enjoy learning about those things in which they are interested *and when children genuinely do want to learn then sooner or later they will*. If participation is to be gained, then it is important to secure a child's interest from the start of the lesson, and therefore 'starters' for science lessons are particularly stressed in Part II of the book.

If children's needs are both cognitive and affective, should this influence our approach to teaching maths and science? Take, for example, 'science'. For many children this is more than just another school subject – it is an adventure in imagination, fired and sustained by innumerable television series and films that glamorise the investigational aspects of scientists' work. For them, science may be the key to open up new worlds, conjuring up images of intrepid explorers discovering lost cities in a steamy jungle or star ship crews charting new regions of outer space. As teachers we should exploit this romantic view rather than discourage it, however remote from reality such ideas may be, for this is where young children's interests initially lie, and it is from these notions we should begin our teaching of science.

It might be argued that topics such as outer space do not allow objects to be brought into the classroom and handled in the same way as more mundane materials but this should in no way detract from thinking and learning about a subject, scientific or otherwise. For example, the greater part of history can only be studied in the primary school from secondary sources – a point well made by Paul Black (1980). One of the most successful infant science projects I have observed was in a school where the classroom had been turned into a solar system, complete with mobiles of planets, comets and the Milky Way. A filmstrip was shown, parents were asked to recall first hearing about the landing on the moon and the project culminated in a visit to the local radio telescope, Jodrell Bank. Most of the learning that took place (and there was much) was in a sense factual but even children who had difficulty with conceptual learning learned a great deal about space. This enabled them to discuss on equal terms with their peers the finer points of what space travel *might* be like. Admittedly the principles of, for example, radio astronomy were beyond the understanding of the children (and some even beyond that of the teachers!) but all in all the project contributed to a total experience that would not easily be forgotten. Knowledge of 'popular science' need not always be seen as the prerogative of the more able, but should provide a focal point of interest for *all* children.

Although children's views of mathematics may be rather more prosaic, Edith Biggs (1985, p. 48), after working with slower learning children, comes to the conclusion that 'Perhaps motivating the children is the most important single factor in securing their attention.' Games and puzzles are enjoyed by almost all children and if these were seen to be part of mathematics from an early age then undoubtedly a more enthusiastic reception to the subject would be generated. It is for this reason that many games and puzzles are included in the central section of this book.

A SPECIAL CURRICULUM IN MATHS AND SCIENCE?

'How would the inclusion of a child with special needs affect the content of my scheme of work?' This question is perhaps uppermost in the minds of many teachers reading this book. The Warnock Report stated that an important factor in determining the success of special educational provision in ordinary schools is the degree to which schools can modify their curriculum to accommodate different groups of children with special needs without detriment to the quality of education offered to other children in the school (DES, 1978, para. 11.10). This is the pattern for an integrated school as it is usually conceived. For example, J. Fish (1985, p. 57) sees the aim of special educational arrangements in ordinary schools as 'to maintain in the school as many children as possible with disabilities and significant difficulties, by providing various combinations of personal support to individual children and their teachers, special materials and special teaching'.

However, special teaching for a special group of children within the same classroom as other children can sometimes fall short of the ideal of integration although in many situations it may be the only practical solution. Those who have attempted to organise such a classroom will know the many problems, not only of time and resources but also of keeping that close community spirit between the members of a class that is so rewarding and possibly unique to primary school teaching. It is widely accepted that less able children should be taught at a less abstract level and at a generally slower pace. However, matching teaching to one or two children while retaining the interest and motivation of the rest of the class is a formidable teaching task. Teaching in a one-to-one situation is rarely possible for any length of time and setting too much individual work for a prolonged session can only increase a less able child's existing sense of isolation. The *Low Attainers in Mathematics 5–16* project suggested that 'the younger low attainers would benefit from following a curriculum broadly similar to that for other pupils but that they should progress through it more slowly and have more experiences leading to each idea' (Denvir, Stolz and Brown, 1982). The aim of the mathematical and scientific ideas presented in this book is to maintain this integrated class social-unit as far as possible while at the same time attempting to provide all children with activities appropriate to their level of understanding.

In a recent report (DES, 1985), HMI stress that the content of the curriculum needs to be differentiated in order to match the different abilities of pupils, but if this is not to act as a straitjacket on the progress of other pupils, activities should be chosen that can be adapted to suit the different levels of maturity and understanding of pupils. They provide an example of an investigatory activity that can be used with a wide range of ages and abilities of children, the value of this being that the differentiation is determined largely by the abilities of the pupils and is not predetermined by the teacher.

Within a book such as this that attempts to deal with the broad subject areas of both mathematics and science, no attempt has been made to provide any substantial contribution to the *content* of these subjects except in relation to planning and evaluation (Part III). It is intended, however, that the ideas in Part II should be used to stimulate the interest of children and so encourage mathematical and scientific thinking. Alternatively, the ideas can be used as starting points for wider mathematical and scientific activities.

The criteria according to which the activities have been chosen are as follows.

1. The activity should involve mathematical or scientific thinking.
2. The idea should have enough flexibility to be adaptable to more than one level of learning.
3. The activity must be sufficiently motivating for children to want to carry it out.

If teaching and learning is to be efficient, we need constantly to evaluate the results of our endeavours and in Chapters 6 and 7 some suggestions are given as to how this might be carried out.

In the final chapter, several different teaching strategies are discussed for children with specific problems in particular areas of mathematics. The ideas and suggestions presented here are offered in the hope that they will prove to be as adaptable to the various teaching styles of teachers as they have been to the differing learning needs of children.

2

Fostering early mathematical and scientific ideas

LEARNING TO THINK

The ability to think rationally does not develop in isolation from the environment. Children who have been brought up apart from human society have invariably shown a retarded rate of social, emotional and intellectual development. This suggests that human reasoning will only develop in an environment conducive to purposeful thinking. From a study of case histories of feral children we can also trace the subsequent development of human emotions such as laughing and crying that were absent in the children when first discovered. The relationship between affectivity and cognition is a subtle but intimate one and particularly in the first few years of a child's life, feelings and emotions dominate all facets of cognitive behaviour. Only gradually do external stimuli displace internal sensations as the primary source of knowledge of the external world. Sensations arising from both internal and external perceptions give rise to actions, and through their actions children at last begin to influence the environment that has so far shaped their lives. It is from the effects of these actions that children construct an initial understanding of the world in which they find themselves.

Symbolism

Much of young children's behaviour imitates actions and events that occur around them. Initially, imitation is carried out in the presence of the model (for example, a response to a hand wave), but later this imitation becomes deferred; that is to say, it can now be performed in the absence of the imitated model. By about 18 months old, this imitative behaviour is internalised and takes the form we know as mental imagery. By this means children are able to 'imitate' objects that are no longer present to the senses but which may be 'imaged', that is to say, imagined. This emerging 'semiotic function' (Piaget, 1969) is the basis of all later forms of symbolism and, in addition to its more obvious role in the development of language, is of considerable importance for mathematical and scientific thinking.

The crucial part played by internal imagery of sight and also of sound in the development of young children is tragically seen in the case of the deaf and blind American girl, Helen Keller. It was at the crucial age of about 18 months when Helen was struck down by an illness from which she only barely recovered. Writing of those early months in her autobiography, she says:

> These happy days did not last long. One brief Spring, musical with the song of robin and mocking-bird, one Summer rich in fruit and roses, one Autumn of gold and crimson sped by and left their gifts at the feet of an eager, delighted child. Then, in the dreary month of February, came the illness which closed my eyes and ears and plunged me into the unconsciousness of an unborn baby . . . Early one morning, however, the fever left me as suddenly and as mysteriously as it had come. There was great rejoicing in the family that morning, but no one, not even the doctor, knew that I should never see or hear again.
>
> (Keller, 1958)

Despite this crippling blow to her nascent ability to comprehend the meaning of symbols, Helen's subsequent development showed that the operation of her intelligence did not depend exclusively on the quality of her incoming sensory data. For those responsible for the education of handicapped children whose senses may be severely limited this has always been an encouragement to look for, and to use, alternative sensory modes of communication.

In teaching such young severely handicapped children, it is important to know how far their behaviour is based on a truly symbolic understanding of language. American workers with deaf–blind children have described the behaviour of children functioning at a 'symbolic level' as being one of 'freedom of self from having-to-do, from handling, from responding directly to the situation, in being able to stand back and not respond, in being able to consider objects without manipulating them' (Robbins and Stenquist, 1967, p. 50). Thus symbolic understanding allows children to manipulate situations at the level of imagination and so to consider and choose one of various possible alternatives, a crucial part of and indeed the basis of much mathematical and scientific thinking.

Concepts and language

With the development of symbolic functioning comes the capacity to evoke and to manipulate concepts, to reverse actions mentally, both seen and performed, and so finally to reflect upon them. With the acquisition of conceptual thinking comes the ability to understand and to use language. Language can 'fix' emerging concepts and also evoke them. It has a correspondence with both things perceived and also the conceptual world of ideas and imagination. Scientific and mathematical language is a particularly precise form of language, which can draw attention to many less obvious aspects of the environment and to subtle relationships that might otherwise pass unnoticed.

Yet just because of its power and pervasiveness, language can also become a straitjacket from which children cannot escape when they are struggling with new ideas and proffered explanations of the world about them. Piaget (1952a) expressed the complex relationship between language and the ideas expressed by language in the following way: 'Thought creates language but then passes beyond it; but language turns on thought and seeks to imprison it'. It is not therefore a question of whether language determines thought or thought language; each both influences – and is influenced by – the development of the other.

Up to this point, language as an articulated system of concepts is still beyond young children although they may be using a variety of communicative phrases to express their needs. But early concepts have to undergo a long period of development and will initially be inexplicably tied to emotional experiences. For example, because a child understands a word in one context this does not mean he or she will understand it in a totally different context. Still less might his or her *use* of the word correspond with the *understanding* of that word, for children understand far more words than they are capable of using. It is therefore part of the teacher's task to help children to use language as effectively as possible since language and thought are the basis of all subsequent mathematical and scientific thinking.

PLAYING AND LEARNING IN THE PRE-SCHOOL PERIOD

For useful scientific concepts to develop, children must interact with the physical world. The rapidity of their progress to mature mathematical and scientific thinking will depend on the quality and richness of their everyday experiences. These in turn are dependent on the freedom children have to explore the world about them and on the opportunities they are given to handle stimulating and exciting materials. Most children are naturally curious and need little direction as to what to do when introduced to new materials. However, in order to discover the properties of substances they must be allowed to investigate freely, to touch and feel, to pull and stretch, to bend and bite. These are the young child's first attempts to get to know an object – its texture, size, weight and strength. They represent his or her first gropings towards a scientific understanding of the way things are.

It will be useful at this juncture to look at some of the activities that lead to rudimentary mathematical and scientific ideas and which may be carried out with young children in a home environment. For convenience these have been collected together under the headings of Outdoor situations and Indoor play.

Outdoor situations

Many outdoor activities are valuable for young children.

1. *Exploring a garden* is an exciting venture for young children. There is a great deal of scientific and mathematical thinking going on when children are playing with soil, discovering and counting the different kinds of insects and beetles, watching how they move, naming plants and flowers, observing their daily routine of opening and closing and noting the change in height as they grow. Different leaves, ferns and grasses can be collected and a note made of the longest, largest, heaviest or smallest. Textures and colours can be observed and words such as *prickly, smooth, sticky, furry, hollow, solid, heavy, light*, etc., are likely to be used in a natural and enjoyable context.

2. *Play with sand* is an ideal medium for discovering the basic mathematical principles of volume, capacity and weight. Buckets, spades and spoons should be made available together with ice-cream cartons, Smartie tubs, plastic bottles, yoghurt containers, etc. One container full of sand can be poured into another of different shape so that children can see that a quantity of substance remains the same, irrespective of the appearance and shape that the substance may take. Children can be encouraged to play 'games' such as filling one container by using another. Typical questions parents or teachers might ask are, 'How many full Smartie tubes will fill an ice-cream tub?' and 'Can you put four spoons of sand on my dish?' Words such as *more, less, most, heavy, light, plenty, once, twice*, etc., should be used in the appropriate circumstances.

3. *The weather* is another source of mathematical and scientific ideas: 'Today is cold but it's warmer than yesterday' 'Which comes first, the thunder or lightning?' It is important to *pose* questions at this stage, but not necessarily to answer them. Some questions can lead to imaginative and inventive thinking, such as, 'Where does the moon go in the day-time?' 'Why do clouds move?' 'Which is furthest away, the sun or the clouds?' 'Have you ever seen a star during the daytime?' Answers to these questions should not be given too soon if we want children to *think* about them.

4. *Visits to zoos and museums* are always a rich source of stimulation provided that children are allowed to explore them in their own time and way. Allowing children this freedom will provoke *their* questions, the answers to which will be remembered more surely than those to questions adults might raise.

5. *Travelling by road*, children can observe many geometrical shapes ranging from the simple arrays of squares in telephone boxes to cylindrical milk-tankers and pillar-boxes. Estimation of size, time and distance, together with intuitions of perspective, are also involved in any road journey.

6. *Shopping* can become a very valuable mathematical experience when time is taken to point out numbers, money, shapes and measures of all kinds. Opportunity should also be given for children to spend their own money, however small the amount or controlled the situation. When buying clothes, questions may be asked about body measurements ('How tall are you?' 'How long are the sleeves?') and these will draw attention to the need for measurement.

Indoor play

Young children learn many fundamental concepts most efficiently through informal play unrestrained by limitations of time. The following are some of the situations that can lead to mathematical and scientific ideas.

1. *Collecting*. Many forms of useful play can be carried out with groups of similar kinds of objects – small dolls, cars, sets of clothes, stamps, etc., in which natural sorting, ordering and matching activities become appropriate. For example, grouping together items of furniture suitable for each room of a doll's house, putting out clothes in the order a doll is to be dressed or matching each cowboy to a horse. As children grow older these logically important classifying and sorting activities can assume

more sophisticated forms such as doing jigsaws, collecting stamps or listing all the names of animals known in alphabetical order.

2. *Water play*. Bath-time is a particularly suitable time for young children to play with water. By playing with sponges, containers, funnels and tubes children may be led to the idea that the amount of water stays the same, whatever shape of container it is poured into (the mathematical principle of 'conservation'). Even young children can develop a 'feel' for the way in which materials behave that may develop later into a 'mechanical aptitude'. It is through this kind of informal playing that young children learn best.

3. *Questions about time*. Questioning children about the times of television programmes and other habitual routines involves estimating durations of time and a desire to learn how to 'tell the time'.

4. *Dice games*. Dice games such as ludo or snakes and ladders involve children in a great deal of counting and practical understanding of the notions of probability and chance. A 'one-in-six' chance becomes a personal experience when children are waiting for a number 'six' on a die.

5. *Bed-time stories*. The many traditional bed-time stories such as *Snow White and the Seven Dwarfs*, *Goldilocks and the Three Bears* and many others introduce numbers and comparisons in a pleasant and enjoyable context.

DEVELOPING CONCEPTS IN THE SCHOOL

It would be impossible in a book of this size and scope to give a detailed account of the development of even the major features of mathematical or scientific thinking. However, it will be useful to note briefly one or two of the more outstanding features of children's thinking. Several of these examples of children's thinking are taken from the work of Jean Piaget, who, despite recent criticism of his methodological and developmental frameworks, has advanced our understanding of children's thinking more than any other figure this century. Much has been made over the past fifty years of the difference between the reasoning processes of young children and those of adults, but in recent years research has restored a more balanced view, which suggests that some of these differences are due to the adult perspectives from which these researches were conducted.

Differences between adult and childish thinking certainly exist, for a child must undergo a great many experiences before he or she can use those experiences as a basis for reasoning and this collection of 'snapshots' of children's reasoning has intentionally focused on these differences. Outlining these differences does not, however, give a true indication of the extent of concordance between childish and adult thinking. There are many areas of agreement between the two and teachers should note these and build on them whenever possible.

Whilst some of the disparities noted here are clearly due to a lack of cognitive development, others are due more to the different purposes and needs for reasoning processes in the life of the child whose social and emotional world is so different to that of the adult. Piaget, whose views on the extent of 'ego-centrism' of the young child have come under particular criticism, wrote over fifty years ago, 'Logic is not co-extensive with intelligence, but consists of the sum total of rules which intelligence makes use of for its own direction' (Piaget, 1977, p. 386).

It is evident that children do see the world very much from their own point of view and do not always fully appreciate that the knowledge they possess may not be possessed by others. For example, a child may be describing his activities of the previous night to a listener. Part of that account typically might include reference to persons of whom the listener has no knowledge but with whom the child nevertheless assumes the listener is acquainted. Piaget goes further than this and claims that children literally cannot take account of another's point of view. This can be seen, for example, in the next section, where children are asked to describe a model from physically different viewpoints.

Since Piaget's original experiments in this area, other researchers have shown that this inability to 'decentre' in imagination is affected drastically by the meaningfulness of the situation to the child. Many experiments purporting to show the illogical nature of children's reasoning have been contradicted by later experimenters who, instead of using formal test situations, used childlike scenarios involving dolls and other characters with whom young children could identify. The earlier researchers who found children's reasoning powers so radically different from adults' had failed to take into account all the factors *children* found relevant in their experimental situations. We must therefore as teachers exercise caution when setting children logical tasks in which the wording or the situation itself is contrived or unfamiliar to the child. Margaret Donaldson (1978) has presented convincing evidence that once children identify with and therefore understand the motives and intentions of the characters involved in these experimental situations, their reasoning becomes much more 'logical'. She makes the point persuasively that although young children are often unable to conceive (literally) of another person's point of view they are nevertheless able to understand what another person may be *feeling*. Here once again we find evidence for the intimate connection between cognitive ability and emotional states of mind. The following sections give brief examples of some of the more important differences between childish and adult thinking.

Emerging ideas about space and time

To a young child, yesterday is a remembered experience and tomorrow an anticipation of things to come. Children's first concepts of time and space are largely intuitive and based on their personal perceptions of the world. Only gradually, with the emergence of the capacity for symbolic representation, will children be able to imagine situations that are no longer present to the spatial or temporal senses. However, before they are able to conceive of an action done they must first have carried out that action themselves, for it is through interactions with external objects that children build up an inner framework of understanding of the way the physical world behaves. It is this inner world of representations to which our reasoning makes reference and eventually enables children to make logical deductions without reference to physical experience.

Although good imagery is important for many aspects of mathematical thinking, it is not sufficient in itself for effective spatial reasoning, for it is the child's *actions* on objects from which his or her inner logic and reasoning is derived. A child's mind does not copy reality and this can be seen in children's drawings, which reflect their personal viewpoint on the world. Therefore, children draw what they *know* before that which they *see*.

Through a stimulating pre-school environment children will begin to build up more mature concepts of space and time. They know their toys are in the box downstairs – they were put there and they will stay there until someone moves them. Several sophisticated tests claim to assess different aspects of spatial development but these are difficult to carry out under classroom conditions. However, a good general indication of the maturity of children's spatial understanding is their ability to imagine and appreciate a situation from another person's literal point of view.

The following simple 'test' is from Piaget but has been adapted for classroom use in the Nuffield Teacher's Guide, *Checking Up II* (1972). Children should be seated with eyes level to the model layout shown. The layout is mounted on a table and contains a castle, tree and house in the relative positions shown. The teacher moves to different positions around the layout keeping his or her eyes level with the models

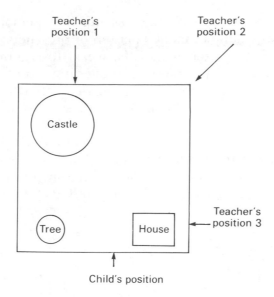

Figure 2.1 *Simple space and time 'test': castle, tree and house*

and asks the child what the teacher can see from the different positions indicated on the diagram (see Figure 2.1). The child is asked to choose from among eight different drawings that represent the objects as seen from different points of view around the table. It is suggested the teacher might say, 'Imagine I am taking a photograph from where I am. What would it look like?' It should be made clear to children that only one picture can be chosen.

Children will often choose the card which represents their own point of view rather than that of the teacher. An alternative form of the task can be to give a single card to children who can then be asked to place themselves in a position so that they can see the same picture that is on the card. The test can be made simpler by restricting the number of positions (and cards) used at any one time. Much can be learnt about the child's understanding of words such as *left*, *right*, *behind*, *in front*, etc., from this sort of situation. However, care must be taken when drawing conclusions about a child's reasoning capacity in view of the rather contrived situation created by this task (see earlier this chapter).

The acquisition of language also plays its part in the development of spatial concepts and lends generality to specific actions and behaviours of the child. It provides names through which children can refer to their growing spatial frame of reference. Language also plays its part in the construction of the child's notions of time by the use of words such as *morning, bedtime, a long time, a short time*, etc. However, for young children time remains essentially a personal and local experience. For example, many children of preschool age may not realise that it is the same day of the week throughout the whole country. Children's understanding of the duration of time also develops gradually – they may not understand that the extent of a duration is independent of the nature of the events that take place in that period of time.

The following example of a task to test children's understanding of time is from Piaget and has been replicated on a number of occasions (for example, Lovell, 1966). Two dolls *A* and *B* are 'raced' on a table in front of a child (see Figure 2.2). They are started at the same time (on

Figure 2.2 *A child's understanding of time: two dolls 'raced' on a table*

hearing a signal) but one doll is moved faster than the other. They are both stopped simultaneously on the sounding of another signal. Although young children admitted that the dolls started at the same time, many claimed that the faster moving doll took a longer time, whereas in fact it had only covered a longer distance. At a later age, children thought that perhaps one doll took more time because it went slower. Others thought that although the dolls started at the same time and took the same time, they didn't stop at the same time.

Clearly these are good reasons for giving children as much experience as possible in dealing with the concepts of time. Relevant classroom activities might include playing at racing electronic 'toys' or noting the distance run by children in a fixed time.

Measuring and counting

When children first choose one object in preference to another they are comparing—for example, *this one makes more noise, that one was sweeter, this one is hotter, that is longer, this is heavier.* Comparison is at the root of all forms of measurement, and children are comparing even before they begin to use words such as *hot, hotter, big, bigger,* etc. However, the words serve to fix these experiences more securely in their minds.

To compare two collections of objects it is sufficient to count the number in each but for materials of a non-discrete or 'continuous' nature (water, sand, etc.) counting is not possible and to decide—for example—which is longer of two rods, children may need to place one length beside the other. This is usually referred to as *direct* comparison. The limitations of this form of measurement are obvious since some objects cannot be physically moved to adjacent positions. Therefore after experience of comparing such objects directly, children should be asked to consider objects that cannot be compared directly. Children will then be led to see the need for an *intermediary* object that can be compared with each of two immovable objects in turn. However, the purpose and use of a 'go-between' object in measuring is not always apparent to children as the following example shows, taken from the writer's own research with children in both ordinary and special schools (Womack, 1983b).

Children were asked which was taller of two tables standing in different corners of the classroom. Since there was no way of comparing the tables directly (i.e. by moving them), children were offered the use of a long stick. It was found that the children used the stick in one of the following three ways.

1. The stick was used in a wand-like fashion, merely as a device to point to each table in turn and to guess which was taller (see Figure 2.3a).
2. The stick was held horizontally and moved across the room from one table to the other whilst attempting to keep the stick at the same height. This showed an inventive use of the stick but was in fact an unsuitable method since the tables differed in height by only a few centimetres (see Figure 2.3b).
3. The stick was taken to one table and the height of the table marked off along the stick with chalk or with the fingers of one hand held in position on the stick. The stick was then carried to the second table and its height compared directly with the marked off section (see Figure 2.3c).

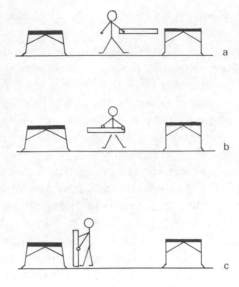

Figure 2.3 *Using a 'go-between' object to assist measurement*

This latter strategy showed a good understanding of an important principle of measuring length – that length is a general property of objects that is independent of the position of that object.

However, direct and indirect comparisons, whether of length, weight, capacity, area, etc., are still only qualitative. If the measuring unit chosen is a small one relative to the item to be measured then quantitative measurement can be carried out to measure, say, how many cupfuls in a pile of seeds or how many plastic counters weigh the same as a lump of Plasticine. This involves counting how many of the smaller unit will make up the larger item. The teaching of counting and number at school traditionally begins with sorting, ordering and matching activities using assortments of different coloured triangles, squares and other miscellaneous items. However, although these activities may be useful for general logical development, they are not directly conducive to the development of counting. Experience of number arises through play with physical objects and therefore when teaching number, children should be encouraged to count, sort and match *collections* of objects. Gradually children realise that the number of objects in a collection remains the same irrespective of the order in which the objects are counted. Piaget called this an understanding of the *conservation* of the number of objects in a collection. (A similar principle is involved with non-countable or 'continuous' quantities. For example, young children may be unsure whether an amount of clay will weigh more or less when it is broken into pieces or deformed into another shape.)

The activity of counting is certainly a most important one but this is adequately dealt with in most primary mathematics schemes. However, the Schools Council Low Attainers Project team made the point that some teaching schemes for young and slow learning children may give too much emphasis to making one-to-one correspondence between objects in sets and consequently to underplay the use of counting (Dickson, Brown and Gibson, 1984). A structured programme for teaching the introduction to counting for slower learners is suggested in Chapter 8 (Example 3).

Language and reasoning

A noticeable feature of children's thinking is observed in their tendency to define an object by a single property or use, rather than attempting to give a more general definition. For example, a child asked, 'What is a television?' might reply, 'We've got a television'. When asked for further clarification, the reply might be given, 'You can watch *Dr Who* on it'.

When children do generalise, it is often to make an inference about *all* cases based on the behaviour or properties of only a few. For example, the reason given by a child for not liking animals may be simply, 'Because they eat you'. The fact that most animals do not eat people is not considered relevant to the answer given. The notion of cause and effect is the basis of scientific thinking but the difference between these two concepts is not always clear to young children. In one of his earliest investigations, Piaget (1930) noted that children may find no contradiction in believing that the wind causes the branches of a tree to move whilst at the same time believing that the branches cause the wind by wafting it along. Piaget also maintained that for young children there are no natural laws; bodies move as they do because they want to and not because they must.

The concept of causation is associated with the word *because*, but care must be taken in teaching the use of this word since it can be used in several different contexts. For example, the square root of 16 is 4 *because* 4 times 4 is 16—a logical context. I'm sitting here *because* I like her!—a psychological context. The solution changed colour *because* I added acid—a scientific or causal context.

Children's use of the word *why* is interesting and often reveals their undeveloped notions of causation. For example, a child's explanation of why a car won't start may be, 'Because it won't move'. If asked why a river flows, a child may reply, 'Because there are fish in it'. There are a whole host of unanswerable *Why* questions children commonly ask, such as, 'Why haven't we got two noses?' or 'Why is my little finger smaller than my middle finger?'—to which an adult can only reply, 'Because it *is*.'

Hypothesising

A common form of reasoning, known as *deductive* reasoning, starts from a general statement and deduces a particular instance from that generalisation. A converse form of argument, *inductive* reasoning, starts from particular facts and moves to a more general statement embracing those facts. Much of children's thinking falls into neither of these categories—it is their tendency to reason from a particular instance to another particular fact. Indeed, they may often make contradictory assertions about the same situation, a mode of thought Piaget calls 'transductive thinking'. For example, asked why a matchstick floats, a young child might reply, 'Because it's small.' Yet later, when asked, 'Why does that ship float?' the same child might reply, 'Because it's big.'

Once children are able to reverse the order of a sequence of events in thought and also in language, it becomes possible for them to consider hypotheses—that is, to imagine and say what they *might* do under certain circumstances. However, care should be taken in the interpretation of what children say they would do, since, like adults, they may not necessarily behave in a practical situation as they say they would in imagination or, for example, if they were a character in a story.

Arriving at an inevitable conclusion from given premises is not easily handled by children. Often their ability to reason in this way is influenced by the nature of the hypothesis from which they start. For example, to ask a child a question that begins 'If I had six fingers . . .' is immediately to put the question beyond the understanding of many children. You *haven't* got six fingers and so the question is neither sensible nor valid from the point of view of the child. Since the question is invalid and so meaningless to children, so the answer is likely to be meaningless to adults.

Children make sense of what is said to them on the basis of the sort of situation in which the language is used—a patently adult way of responding. It is often therefore the less able child's misinterpretation of a situation that leads to an incorrect deduction being made rather than lack of understanding or inability to use a logical rule.

Children do have limitations to the development of their logical thought, primarily due to their tendency to see a problem only from their own point of view and also to a great extent by their own lack of consciousness of their own thinking (introspection). We should not, however, be deterred from encouraging children to explore deeper or more complex ideas, for almost all problems can be eventually understood if sufficient time is devoted to their solution.

The following chapters present a selection of ideas and activities to which all children in primary schools may be introduced with the hope that teachers may be inspired to invent for themselves further classroom activities that foster mathematical and scientific thinking.

PART II
Ideas into Action

3

Thinking mathematically

As teachers we know mathematics to be a concise and powerful means of understanding the world—a symbolic medium of communication that represents and at the same time both explains and predicts the behaviour of things. However, for young children at school, mathematics often appears to be simply the art of counting objects and using structural apparatus to find the answers to numerical problems.

Thinking mathematically implies more than handling materials and manipulating numbers: it is looking for pattern and order, deducing relationships or making predictions and hypotheses. It involves counting and calculating, recording and measuring, generalising and reasoning.

Although in the teaching of mathematics, concrete materials are often necessary for young children if progress is to be made, the essence of mathematical thinking is not the concrete or specific. Somewhat paradoxically, as teachers we have the difficult task of attempting to teach children to think generally and abstractly through the use of specific and concrete materials. How therefore should we go about such a task? The Cockcroft Report (DES, 1982) distinguishes between three distinct aspects in the teaching of mathematics. These are *conceptual structures, facts and skills* and *general strategies*.

Conceptual structures, facts and skills

Conceptual structures lie at the heart of mathematics and most good primary mathematics schemes give adequate attention to these. There is, however, much uncertainty as to how best to teach facts and skills. Cockcroft recommended that 'facts' such as '1 litre equals approximately 1¾ pints') and 'skills' (for example, knowing that 6 + 4 = 10) should be brought up to a level of immediate recall. Attaining such familiarity has many advantages. For example, a knowledge of number facts and skills allows less able children to compete favourably with other children in relatively straightforward arithmetical problems, giving them a much-needed confidence with number. A close familiarity with number facts is also useful if not essential in many mental problem-solving situations and most of the activities in this chapter require children to practise them in the context of more general mathematical thinking. A good acquaintance with the 'nuts and bolts' of algorithms also frees the conscious attention of children to deal with the more general mathematical strategies that may be involved in problem-solving. Indeed in certain circumstances it may well be better for a child to have the skill to perform an algorithm without understanding exactly how it works than not to have the skill at all. It is of course always essential to know *when* to use that 'mechanical' skill. The value of games and other motivating activities to help slower learning children in the memorisation of number facts has been strongly advocated by a number of authorities (for example, Edith Biggs, 1985), and therefore many of the activities in this chapter are presented in the context of game-like situations.

General strategies and investigations

The general strategies referred to by Cockcroft are the sorts of skills used in problem-solving and investigational work. Although a growing number of teachers realise that such work involves more than just the application of arithmetic to practical situations, investigational work continues to be a much neglected part of the maths curriculum in many primary schools. It is often difficult to find a sufficient number of problems that lend themselves to substantial investigation for all the children in a class and, in addition, teachers do not know exactly where the investigation might lead and whether they will have sufficient knowledge to deal with all the questions that might arise. Many investigations are also considered too 'open-ended' for the average pupil and such work is often reserved for more able children. Investigations are generally wider in scope than problem-solving. Typically they consist of open-ended ideas constrained within the framework of a few simple rules or conditions. Some of the activities presented here may be considered 'closed' in so far as they have only one solution but in most cases that solution can be used to generate further topics for investigation. General strategies for both investigations and problem-solving are difficult to pinpoint and can only be successfully practised with specific examples. However, some of the following suggestions for approaching a specific problem may be found useful.

- Try to find a pattern or analogy, in either numbers or shapes.
- Make a diagram whenever possible.

- Try all possibilities exhaustively.
- Be absolutely consistent in applying a rule or condition.
- Try to imagine what the solution would look like.
- Record results systematically – in a table where possible.

A major source of difficulty for many slower learning children is their failure to take into account all the conditions that restrain an investigation and time should be taken to stress the necessity of considering more than one relationship at a time.

In the writer's experience it is not sufficient to present to teachers an investigatory problem with the simple instruction, 'investigate'. The busy teacher needs much more specific information and guidance if the investigation is to be planned successfully for a large and heterogeneous class of children. Full teaching notes for each activity have therefore been included here.

There is a great range of ability in mathematics in most primary school classes. This presents class teachers with an extremely difficult task when preparing lesson material, since teaching a class of children at only one level can soon lose the attention of children at other levels of the learning spectrum. Most of the activities here have therefore been adapted to the needs of children of differing abilities by dividing them into three levels of difficulty. In most cases it will be useful to begin at the simplest level and progress to higher levels at a pace appropriate to the teaching situation.

Exploring numbers with a calculator

Calculators are now used widely in schools and initial fears that their use might affect children's competency in basic skills have now been largely discounted. Children enjoy using them because of their toylike nature and the sense of 'control' they give to the user. They can be used both in the classroom or outdoors (for example, in shopping situations) and provide a useful introduction to work with micro-computers. Their adaptability and portability make them a valuable resource for teachers with a very wide range of ability in their classes and they are particularly useful in a remedial situation or for consolidatory exercises for individual children (for example, in the practice of number facts or number bonds). Since they make no demands on the user and are infinitely 'patient', they can also give confidence to those children prone to make errors in mathematics.

Calculators can also be used to extend number investigations for more able children. Their most valuable mathematical contribution is in the following areas: decimals and their relation to place value; fractions and their relation to division; numerical estimation and approximation; dealing with large numbers; and separating a mathematical strategy from its accompanying arithmetic process. Two calculator activities have therefore been included here.

NUMBER INVESTIGATIONS FOR THE CLASSROOM

Activities can be used at the start or the close of a lesson according to the teaching style of the teacher and should be used to stimulate as much discussion as possible. Most of the investigations require only pencil and paper (occasionally squared paper) and are suitable for whole-class use, group discussion or with individual children. 'Answers' are provided for all the activities for the convenience of teachers and suggestions are given for creating further activities along the lines of those already set down. The activities are as follows:

- Wagon wheels
- Ladders and snakes
- Escalators
- Clock arithmetic
- Star-line sums
- Minefields
- Addition squares
- See-side sums
- Shortcuts
- Magic squares
- Four-in-a-line (calculator)
- Making the most (calculator)

WAGON WHEELS

INTRODUCTION

1. This is a wagon.
The wagon number (7) is the sum
of the two wheel numbers.
So, 7 = 2 + 5

2. What are the wheel numbers
on this wagon?
Answer 0 + 8 or 1 + 7 or 2 + 6
or 3 + 5 or 4 + 4

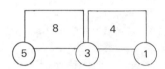

3. This is a wagon train.
The wagon numbers are still
the sum of the wheel numbers.
Therefore, 8 = 5 + 3 and 4 = 3 + 1

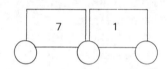

4. Find the wagon wheel numbers
to make this train 'go'.
Answer 6,1,0 or 7,0,1

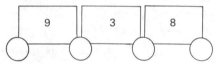

5. Find the wheel numbers
on this wagon train.
(There are four possible solutions.)

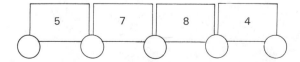

ACTIVITIES

Level 1: wagon trains

Find these wagon wheel numbers:

1. This has several solutions.

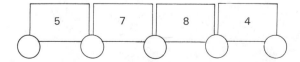

2. This has one solution.

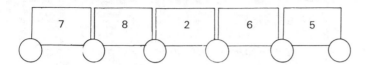

3.

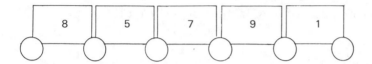

Level 2: wagon rings

Wagons can be linked for defence.
The wheel numbers for this wagon ring are:
1(1)0(3)3(9)6 or 0(1)1(3)2(9)7.
(*Note* The wagon numbers
are printed in brackets.)

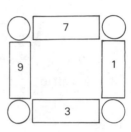

Find the wheel numbers on these wagon rings:

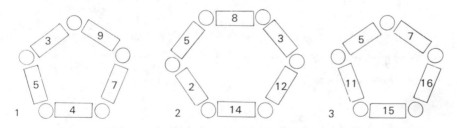

Level 3: wagon triangles

Find the wheel numbers on these wagon triangles:

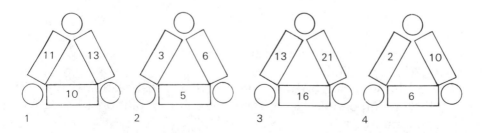

INVESTIGATIONS

Level 1

Solve these four-sided wagon rings (wagon squares). The wagon numbers are given in a clockwise direction. (f) is shown here.

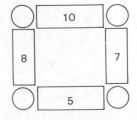

(a) 6, 9, 7, 4   (b) 8, 10, 6, 4
(c) 10, 7, 6, 9   (d) 9, 12, 8, 5
(e) 11, 13, 7, 5   (f) 10, 7, 5, 8

Now add opposite pairs of wagon numbers. What do you notice?

Level 2

Complete the following table for the wagon squares:

	Square a	Square b	Square c
Sum of two opposite wagon numbers			
Total of all four wheel numbers			

Level 3

Complete the following table for the wagon triangles:

	Triangle 1	Triangle 2	Triangle 3	Triangle 4
Total of wagon numbers				
Total of wheel numbers				

TEACHING NOTES FOR WAGON WHEELS

SOLUTIONS TO ACTIVITIES (*Note* Wagon numbers are printed in brackets):

Level 1

1. For example, 2(5)3(7)4(8)4(4)0
2. 0(7)7(8)1(2)1(6)5(5)0
3. Since the 5th wheel is 0 or 1, the 4th wheel must be greater than 7, which is impossible. Therefore there is no solution in positive whole numbers.

Level 2

1. (3)2(9)7(7)0(4)4(5)1 (One solution only.)
2. (8)3(3)0(12)12(14)2(2)0(5)5 (One solution only.)
3. (5)0(7)7(16)9(15)6(11)5 (One solution only.)

Level 3

1. (11)7(13)6(10)4
2. (3)2(6)4(5)1
3. (13)9(21)12(16)4
4. No solution in positive whole numbers.

SOLUTIONS TO INVESTIGATIONS

Level 1

The sum of opposite pairs of wagon numbers is the same.

Level 2

The sum of any opposite pair of wagon numbers equals the sum of all four wheel numbers. (An algebraic solution can be shown to more capable children as follows: if wheel numbers are a, b, c, d, then wagon numbers are $a+b$, $b+c$, $c+d$, $d+a$. The sum of opposite wagon numbers is the same in each of the two cases, namely $a+b+c+d$. This is also the sum of the wheel numbers.)

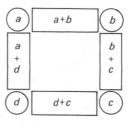

Level 3

The total of the wagon numbers is always twice that of the wheel numbers.

Notes

1. Wagon rings with an odd number of wagons have a unique (single) solution if they have one at all in positive whole numbers.

2. Wagon rings with an even number of wagons have a solution if the sum of the odd-positioned wagon numbers equals the sum of the even-positioned wagon numbers. For example, for four-sided

rings, the sum of each pair of opposite wagon numbers will be the same.

3. A general strategy for solving wagon triangles is to begin with the largest possible number at one corner. As this figure is decreased by 1, the total at the two other corners increases by 2. Decrease the figure in the initial corner until the total of the other two corners equals the required number between them. Let children find their own strategies initially. Then discuss better strategies. Beginning with the smallest wagon number is a good strategy.

4. More wagon trains and rings can be simply constructed by beginning with the wagon *wheels*, calculating the wagon numbers, then erasing the wheel numbers. *Small* wagon numbers in trains or rings allow fewer possible answers.

LADDERS AND SNAKES

INTRODUCTION

This is a ladder that started with
the two numbers 3 and 4.
3+4=7, 4+7=11, 7+11=18, 11+18=29.
Therefore the next number between
the rungs of the ladder is 29.

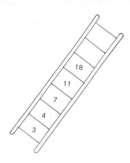

ACTIVITIES

Level 1: ladders

Try to complete these ladders, 1+4=5, 4+5=9, 5+9=

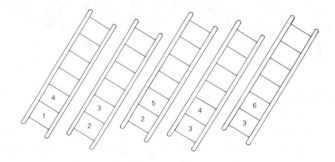

Level 2: snakes

These are snakes. They finish up the same as ladders but you begin
from the *end* first. For example, 18−11=7, 11−7=4, 7−4=3. So the
first snake is 18 11 7 4 3. Can you *complete* these snakes?

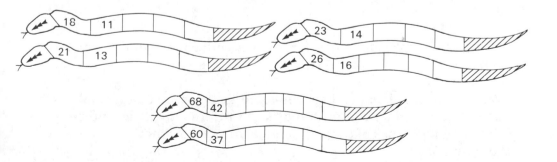

Level 3: ladders and snakes

Complete these ladders and snakes by putting in the missing numbers.

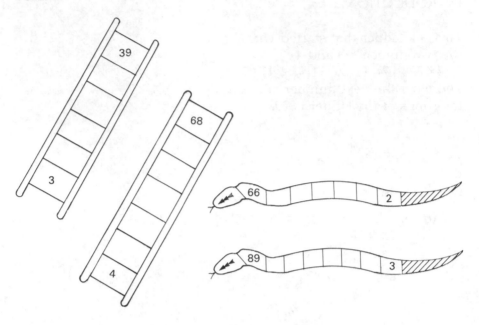

TEACHING NOTES FOR LADDERS AND SNAKES

1. Both ladders and snakes can be made of any length and size of numbers beginning with any two numbers, repeatedly added. Tables of possible ladders can be made as follows (direction of ladder development is left to right):

```
0  1  1  2  3   5   8  13  ...
0  2  2  4  6  10  16  ...
0  3  3  6  ...
...
1  1  2  3  5  ...
1  2  3  5  ...
1  3  4  7  ...
```

Using these tables, teachers can produce numerous ladder or snake puzzles to any level of difficulty.

2. A game of ladders and snakes could be devised so that children landing on a ladder complete the ladder before moving *up* and children landing on a snake must complete the snake if they do not wish to move *down*.

SOLUTIONS TO ACTIVITIES

Level 1

1,4,5,9,14,23
2,3,5,8,13,21
2,5,7,12,19,31
3,4,7,11,18,29
3,6,9,15,24,39

Level 2

18,11,7,4,3
21,13,8,5,3
23,14,9,5,4
26,16,10,6,4,2
68,42,26,16,10,6,4,2
60,37,23,14,9,5,4,1

Level 3

3,6,9,15,24,39
66,41,25,16,9,7,2
4,6,10,16,26,42,68
89,55,34,21,13,8,5,3

Note
The first series of numbers (0 1 1 2 3 5 8 . . .) is known as the Fibonacci series. In any ladder, if any number is divided by the following number, the fraction obtained grows closer and closer to 0.61803 . . ., known as the *Golden Ratio*. The higher up the ladder from which the numbers are obtained, the closer this ratio grows to this *non-terminating decimal number, symbolised as* Φ *(phi)*. For example, take the ladder 4 7 11 18 29 47 . . .:

$$4/7 = 0.57 \ldots \quad 7/11 = 0.636 \ldots$$
$$11/18 = 0.611 \ldots \quad 18/29 = 0.620 \ldots \quad 29/47 = 0.617 \ldots$$

This property can be used to solve long ladders and snakes problems. For further details of 'Phi, the Golden Ratio' see Martin Gardner's *More Mathematical Puzzles and Diversions* (Penguin, 1966).

ESCALATORS

INTRODUCTION

This is the start of an escalator.
The number at the top of the
escalator is 7.

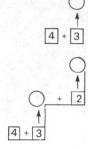

Here is another escalator.
The missing numbers are 7 and 9.
Write these numbers in the circles.

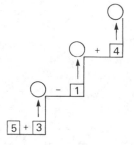

Here is another escalator.
Fill in the missing numbers.
(The numbers are 8, 7 and 11.)

ACTIVITIES

Level 1

Fill in the missing numbers in the staircases of these escalators. The
missing staircase numbers are 1,2,3,4,5. (The first staircase number
(2) has already been inserted in example 1.)

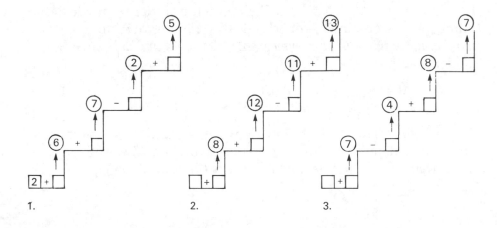

1.   2.   3.

Level 2

Fill in the missing staircase numbers in these escalators. The missing numbers are 1,2,3,4,5. Find the first two staircase numbers. (*Hint* Try 5.) Then you can complete the circles, but you must start from the bottom of the staircase.

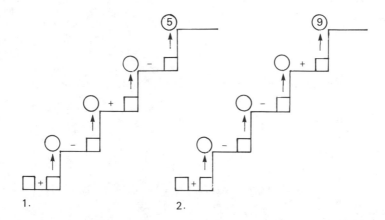

1. 2.

Level 3

This is called a *proper* escalator. It uses each of the four processes +, −, ×, ÷ once only.

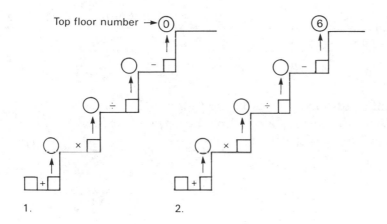

1. 2.

1. Fill in the missing staircase numbers 1,2,3,4,5 to make a *top floor* escalator number of 0.

2. Fill in the missing staircase numbers 1,2,3,4,5 to make a *top floor* escalator number of 6.

3. Fill in the missing staircase numbers 2,3,4,5,6 in more proper escalators to make *top floor* escalator numbers of:
(a) 7
(b) 10

4. Fill in the missing staircase numbers 3,4,5,6,7 in a proper escalator to make a *top floor* escalator number of 8.

INVESTIGATIONS

1. Solve the *proper* escalator in Level 3 using the numbers:

(a) 4, 5, 6, 7, 8
(b) 5, 6, 7, 8, 9
(c) 6, 7, 8, 9, 10

(*Note* The *top floor number* must be a whole number.)

2. Complete the following tables:

Numbers used	1–5	2–6	3–7	4–8	5–9	6–10	7–11	8–12
Top floor escalator number	0	1						

Numbers used	1–5	2–6	3–7	4–8	5–9	6–10	7–11	8–12
Top floor escalator number	6	7	8					

What do you notice?

3. Find solutions using only the numbers 1 to 5 to this special escalator when the *top floor* numbers are (a) 7 (b) 1.

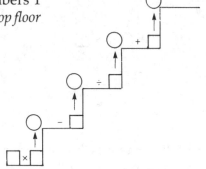

4. Make up your own escalators using any of the four processes, +, −, ×, ÷.

TEACHING NOTES FOR ESCALATORS

Note Ensure the children understand that the given staircase numbers are always inserted into the 'staircase' and that the numbers in the circles are determined by these staircase numbers.

SOLUTIONS TO ACTIVITIES

(Solutions are given in ascending order.)

Level 1

1. 4, 1, 5, 3
2. 3, 5, 4, 1, 2
3. 5, 2, 3, 4, 1

Level 2 (numbers in boxes only)

1. 1, 4, 2, 5, 3 or 5, 4, 3, 1, 2
2. 5, 3, 1, 2, 4 (for example)

Level 3 (numbers in boxes only)

1. 1, 5, 2, 3, 4 or 1, 5, 2, 4, 3
2. 1, 3, 5, 2, 4
3.(a) 2, 4, 6, 3, 5
   (b) 5, 3, 4, 2, 6
4. 3, 5, 7, 4, 6

SOLUTIONS TO INVESTIGATIONS

1.(a) 4, 8, 5, 6, 7... to top floor number 3
  (b) 5, 9, 6, 7, 8... to top floor number 4
  (c) 6, 10, 7, 8, 9... to top floor number 5

2.

Numbers used	1−5	2−6	3−7	4−8	5−9	...$a \to (a+4)$
Top floor escalator number	6	7	8	9	10	$a+5$

or

Numbers used	1–5	2–6	3–7	4–8	5–9	...$a \to (a+4)$
Top floor escalator number	0	1	2	3	4	$a-1$

(These relations can be shown algebraically for the five numbers a, $a+1$, $a+2$, $a+3$, $a+4$ as indicated in the general term for each table.)

3.(a) 5, 4, 2, 3, 1
　(b) 3, 4, 2, 5, 1

CLOCK ARITHMETIC

INTRODUCTION

The following are four games for individual children based on the playing-card game of *Clock*. Each game deals with one of the four processes and therefore can be played at a level of difficulty appropriate to the child's progress in basic arithmetic.

ACTIVITIES

Level 1: Seven-up

This game teaches the addition facts from 1 to 7.

Materials required
Thirty-five flash cards of any size containing the addition facts from 1 to 7 on one side (see below). The reverse side of the cards are blank. A board can easily be made from cardboard to aid in positioning the cards for those children who need it (although this is not essential).

			Position			
1	2	3	4	5	6	7
0+1	0+2	0+3	0+4	0+5	0+6	0+7
1+0	1+1	1+2	1+3	1+4	1+5	1+6
	2+0	2+1	2+2	2+3	2+4	2+5
		3+0	3+1	3+2	3+3	3+4
			4+0	4+1	4+2	4+3
				5+0	5+1	5+2
					6+0	6+1
						7+0

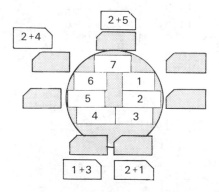

To play

The cards are shuffled and dealt face downwards around the 'clock' dial in the positions 1 to 7 as shown above. Two cards are dealt in position 1, three cards in position 2, four cards in position 3, etc. The final card dealt to position 7 is turned up. This card is then placed adjacent to the pile of cards in the position equal to its sum and the top card in that pile turned over. For example, the card 1+3 would be placed in position 4. If the card taken from position 4 is 2+5, then this is placed adjacent to position 7, etc.

Play is continued in this way until a card is placed adjacent to a position that has no unturned cards left. At this point the game ends. Children are strongly motivated to repeat the game until all the cards have been turned over during one game session.

(*Note* Cutting a small right-hand corner off the top of each card will ensure the cards are kept the same way up.)

Level 2: Nine-up (subtraction)

A similar game to Seven-up with the following changes. Forty-five flash cards are used containing all the subtraction facts involving two-digit numbers less than 20 and single-digit numbers that give a single-digit answer (zero excepted)—see below. There are nine positions for the cards (see below). One card is dealt in position 1, two cards in position 2, etc.

Subtraction fact cards required:

				Position				
1	2	3	4	5	6	7	8	9
								18–9
							17–9	17–8
						16–9	16–8	16–7
					15–9	15–8	15–7	15–6
				14–9	14–8	14–7	14–6	14–5
			13–9	13–8	13–7	13–6	13–5	13–4
		12–9	12–8	12–7	12–6	12–5	12–4	12–3
	11–9	11–8	11–7	11–6	11–5	11–4	11–3	11–2
10–9	10–8	10–7	10–6	10–5	10–4	10–3	10–2	10–1

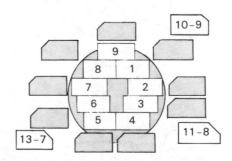

Level 3: Nine-up (division)

The same game as Nine-up with the following changes. Forty-five flash cards are used containing the following division facts from 2 to 10 (omitting division by 0 and 1)—see below. There are nine positions for the cards. One card is dealt in position 1, two cards in position 2, etc. Play proceeds as for subtraction Nine-up.

				Position				
1	2	3	4	5	6	7	8	9
2÷2	4÷2	6÷2	8÷2	10÷2	12÷2	14÷2	16÷2	18÷2
	6÷3	9÷3	12÷3	15÷3	18÷3	21÷3	24÷3	27÷3
		12÷4	16÷4	20÷4	24÷4	28÷4	32÷4	36÷4
			20÷5	25÷5	30÷5	35÷5	40÷5	45÷5
				30÷6	36÷6	42÷6	48÷6	54÷6
					42÷7	49÷7	56÷7	63÷7
						56÷8	64÷8	72÷8
							72÷9	81÷9
								90÷10

Children should be allowed to consult 'tables' for any of the games if this aids enjoyable playing of the game.

Nine-up (multiplication)

This is played in the same way as division Nine-up using the forty-five cards shown (see below). One card is dealt in position 1, two cards in position 2, etc.

				Position				
1	2	3	4	5	6	7	8	9
1×?=1	1×?=2	1×?=3	1×?=4	1×?=5	1×?=6	1×?=7	1×?=8	1×?=9
	2×?=4	2×?=6	2×?=8	2×?=10	2×?=12	2×?=14	2×?=16	2×?=18
		3×?=9	3×?=12	3×?=15	3×?=18	3×?=21	3×?=24	3×?=27
			4×?=16	4×?=20	4×?=24	4×?=28	4×?=32	4×?=36
				5×?=25	5×?=30	5×?=35	5×?=40	5×?=45
					6×?=36	6×?=42	6×?=48	6×?=54
						7×?=49	7×?=56	7×?=63
							8×?=64	8×?=72
								9×?=81

STAR-LINE SUMS

INTRODUCTION

This is a star-line sum.
The three numbers in the horizontal and
vertical lines each total 8
(i.e. 4+1+3=8, 5+1+2=8).
The numbers used are 1,2,3,4,5.
These are called the star numbers.
The star-sum is 8.

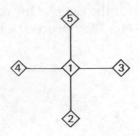

ACTIVITIES

Level 1

1.(a) Use only the star numbers
1,2,3,4,5 to make a star-sum of 9.
(b) Use the same numbers to make
a star-sum of 10.

2. Use the star numbers 2,3,4,5,6.
Make star-sums of:

(a) 11
(b) 12
(c) 13

3. Use the star numbers 3,4,5,6,7.
Make star-sums of:

(a) 14
(b) 15
(c) 16

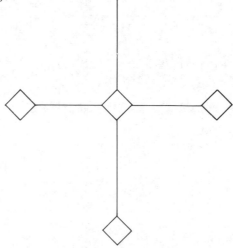

INVESTIGATION

Complete the following table:

Star numbers	1–5	2–6	3–7	4–8	5–9	6–10	7–11	8–12
Possible star-sums	8	11	14					
	9	12	15					
	10	13	16					

Level 2

1. Use the numbers 1,2,3,4,5,6,7 in this six-pointed star. Make star-sums of:

(a) 10
(b) 12
(c) 14

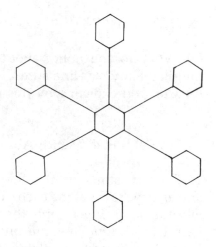

2. Use the numbers 2,3,4,5,6,7,8. Make star-sums of:

(a) 13
(b) 15
(c) 17

INVESTIGATION

Complete the following table:

Star numbers	1–7	2–8	3–9	4–10	5–11	6–12	7–13	8–14
Possible star-sums	10	13						
	12	15						
	14	17						

Level 3

1. Use the numbers 1 to 9 in
this eight-pointed star.
Make star-sums of:

(a) 12
(b) 15
(c) 18

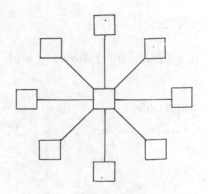

2. Can you make up your own star-line sums
for a star with ten points?

INVESTIGATION

(a) What do you notice about the numbers that always go in the
middle of any star-line sum?
(b) Can you explain why this is?

ACTIVITIES FOR MORE ABLE CHILDREN

1. The star-sums of this hexagon
and also the totals along each side are
all equal to 21. It uses only the numbers 1 to 13. One line and one side
have been already completed. Complete the other numbers.

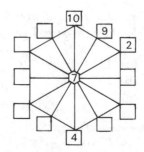

2. The total along each *side* of these stars should equal the number in
the middle. You can use any numbers. Some of the numbers have
been given. You must calculate the remaining numbers.

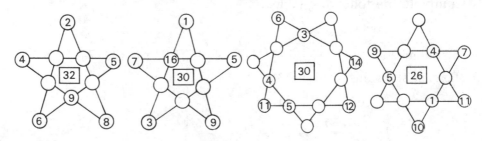

TEACHING NOTES FOR STAR-LINE SUMS

SOLUTIONS TO ACTIVITIES

Level 1

1. (a) 4+3+2=9   5+3+1=9
   (b) 4+5+1=10   3+5+2=10
2. (a) 6+2+3=11   5+2+4=11
   (b) 5+4+3=12   6+4+2=12
   (c) 4+6+3=13   5+6+2=13
3. (a) 7+3+4=14   6+3+5=14
   (b) 6+5+4=15   7+5+3=15
   (c) 5+7+4=16   6+7+3=16

Level 2

1. (a) 3+1+6=2+1+7=4+1+5=10
   (b) 1+4+7=2+4+6=3+4+5=12
   (c) 1+7+6=2+7+5=3+7+4=14
2. (a) 4+2+7=3+2+8=5+2+6=13
   (b) 2+5+8=3+5+7=4+5+6=15
   (c) 2+8+7=3+8+6=4+8+5=17

Level 3

1. (a) 2+1+9=3+1+8=4+1+7=5+1+6=12
   (b) 1+5+9=2+5+8=3+5+7=4+5+6=15
   (c) 1+9+8=2+9+7=3+9+6=4+9+5=18

SOLUTIONS TO INVESTIGATIONS

Level 1

Star numbers	1–5	2–6	3–7	4–8	5–9	6–10	7–11	8–12
Possible star-sums	8	11	14	17	20	23	26	29
	9	12	15	18	21	24	27	30
	10	13	16	19	22	25	28	31

Level 2

Star numbers	1–7	2–8	3–9	4–10	5–11	6–12	7–13	8–14
Possible star-sums	10	13	16	19	22	25	28	31
	12	15	18	21	24	27	30	33
	14	17	20	23	26	29	32	35

Level 3

The first, last or middle star number always goes in the middle—to leave 'balancing' pairs of numbers on either side.

SOLUTION TO ACTIVITIES FOR MORE ABLE CHILDREN

1. Clockwise round the figure: 10, 9, 2, 13, 6, 11, 4, 5, 12, 1, 8, 3

MINEFIELDS

INTRODUCTION

These are minefields divided into plots of land. The number of mines in each plot of land has been given inside the plot. You must make your way across each minefield passing through as small a number of mines as possible. You cannot cross at the corners of minefields. Begin in the square with a gap. For example, the safest way to cross this minefield is: 5 to 6 to 4 to 2 to 3 as shown. This route passes through only 20 mines (5+6+4+2+3=20).

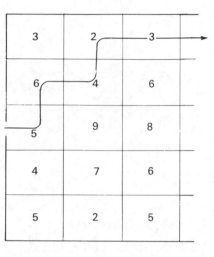

ACTIVITIES

Level 1

Try these minefields. Which route across the minefield has the lowest total?

2	4	5	8
7	1	9	7
5	9	6	9
5	3	8	7
3	2	9	5

2	6	4	5
3	8	2	3
5	9	3	6
5	2	6	4
4	3	5	1

Level 2

Now you can only cross the minefields at the *corners* of each plot. (You cannot enter a plot with a whole side adjacent to your plot.)

Start in any square on the left of the field. For example, one route is 5 to 8 to 3 to 4. This has a total of 20. Is there a better route with a smaller total?

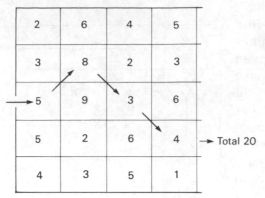

1	5	2	4	6	3
3	6	3	7	5	7
5	4	4	5	2	2
4	2	7	3	3	6
6	1	5	6	4	4

Level 3: Berlin Wall

You are at the bottom of the wall and you must escape to the top of the wall. You must chisel out bricks to make a hole from the bottom to the top. The number of *minutes* it takes to remove each brick is given. What is the fastest time it takes you to break through the wall? For example, one way is 5 to 3 to 6 to 5. This takes a total of 19 minutes. Can you find a better way?

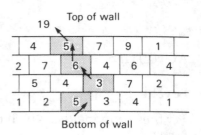

INVESTIGATIONS

Level 1

Make up your own minefields of more than five lines wide.

Level 2

Make up your own corner-gate minefields.

Level 3

Make up your own Berlin Walls.

TEACHING NOTES FOR MINEFIELDS

Levels 1, 2 and 3

If a die or other means is used to create random numbers, then similar examples of minefields and Berlin Walls can easily be made by the children themselves and played with a partner.

Level 3

A Berlin Wall matrix can be made by using a thick black pen or pencil over faintly printed graph-paper. By photocopying the resultant wall or by using a heat-copier directly, either a Banda spirit-master or an ink stencil can be produced.

ADDITION SQUARES

INTRODUCTION

This is an addition square.

+	3	5
8		
4		

This is the solution.

+	3	5
8	11	13
4	7	9

The first addition square is not complete. The square has been completed by adding the corresponding inner numbers as shown.

ACTIVITIES

Level 1

Complete these addition squares.

1.

+	2	7
3		
5		

2.

+	3	1	4
6			
2			
5			

3.

+	7	1	4	9
6				
3				
8				
2				

Level 2

This addition square was completed but the outer numbers were rubbed out.

We can fill them in again in two ways.

+		
	1	5
	6	10

+	1	5
0	1	5
5	6	10

or

+	0	4
1	1	5
6	6	10

Complete these addition squares.

1.

+		
	16	8
	10	2

2.

+		
	3	12
	6	15

3.

+		
	11	13
	9	11

4.

+		
	5	7
	12	14

Level 3

1.

+			
	16	8	9
	10	2	3
	15	7	8

2.

+			
	3	12	8
	6	15	11
	8	17	13

3.

+			
	11	7	13
	4	0	6
	9	5	11

4.

+				
	5	2	7	3
	4	1	6	2
	7	4	9	5
	11	8	13	9

INVESTIGATIONS

Level 2

1.(a) Can you complete this addition square?

+		
	5	8
	7	6

(b) Look at solutions to your other addition squares. What do you notice? Here are four completed squares for examples.

+	0	1
0	0	1
1	1	2

+	0	1
1	1	2
2	2	3

+	0	5
5	5	10
0	0	5

+	1	3
1	2	4
7	8	10

Level 3

1. Can you make up 3×3 squares which can be completed?
2. Can you make up 4×4 squares which can be completed?

A trick with addition squares
Make up your own addition square. Add up all the numbers round the edges and write the sum down. Ask a friend to put one coin (*) in each row and each column (for example, you will need three coins for a 3×3 square).

+	7	9	2	5	4
3	*	12	5	8	7
8	15	17	10	*	12
1	8	*	3	6	5
6	13	15	*	11	10
0	7	9	2	5	*

Without looking at the numbers your friend has covered, ask him to add all the covered numbers and write the answer down. You can tell him the number he has written. It will be the number *you* first wrote down. Try it with a really big addition square!

TEACHING NOTES FOR ADDITION SQUARES

SOLUTIONS TO ACTIVITIES

Level 1

These addition squares can be easily made to any level of difficulty. Subtraction squares can also be made but require a rule that the column number is always subtracted from the row number.

Level 2

Outer numbers are given in the order: row numbers (left to right), followed by column numbers (top to bottom). One solution only is given.

1. 8, 0; 8, 2, etc.   2. 0, 9; 3, 6, etc.   3. 0, 2; 11, 9, etc.   4. 0, 2; 5, 12, etc.

Level 3

1. 10, 2, 3; 6, 0, 5, etc.   2. 2, 11, 7; 1, 4, 6, etc.   3. 4, 0, 6; 7, 0, 5, etc.   4. 3, 0, 5, 1; 2, 1, 4, 8, etc.

SOLUTIONS TO INVESTIGATIONS

Level 2

1.(a) No solution is possible.

(b) The sum of each diagonally opposite pair of digits inside the square is the same.

$+$	a	b
c	$a+c$	$b+c$
d	$a+d$	$b+d$

This is always true, since algebraically for any outer numbers a, b, c, d, the inner numbers are $a+c$, $b+c$, $a+d$, $b+d$. The sums of diagonally opposite inner numbers are $(a+c) + (b+d)$ and $(b+c) + (a+d)$. Each of these is equal to the sum of all the four outer numbers.

Level 3

+			
	A	*B*	*C*
	D	*E*	*F*
	G	*H*	*I*

1. In a 3×3 addition square, it can be shown algebraically that the sum of the digits in the two diagonal lines must be equal. In other words, $A+I=C+G$, $A+E=B+D$, $B+F=E+C$, $D+H=E+G$, $E+I=F+H$.

2. A 4×4 square contains a number of 2×2 addition squares (with the property that the sum of each diagonally opposite pair of digits inside the square is the same). Children can be asked to find these 2×2 squares.

   The 4×4 square also contains four 3×3 addition squares; 5×5 squares and higher have similar properties and these could be made the basis of an investigation by more able children.

The trick

This works because the coins always cover all the sums of all the pairs of outer numbers once only (i.e. $7+3, 9+1, 2+6, 5+8, 4+0$)—but this is the sum of all the outer numbers, i.e. $(7+9+2+5+4) + (3+8+1+6+0)$.

Notes

1. The number of solutions to any square is *one more than the lowest number in the square's inner matrix*. For example, this square will have four solutions corresponding to the digits 3, 2, 1, 0 in the top left position. This applies to *any* size of square.

+		
	3	7
	10	14

2. More addition squares are easily constructed by selecting any set of outer numbers first, completing the square, then deleting the outer numbers. Let children begin with squares that have many solutions.

SEE-SIDE SUMS

INTRODUCTION

Can you insert the numbers 0, 1, 2, 3, 4, 5 into the circles to make a total of 6 along each side of this triangle?

Solution:

1+5+0=6
0+4+2=6
2+3+1=6

ACTIVITIES

Level 1

1. Put the numbers 0 to 5 in this triangle to make a total of 9 along each side.

2. Put the numbers 1 to 6 in the triangle to make a total of 9.

3. Put the numbers 1 to 6 in the triangle to make a total of 12.

4. Put the numbers 2 to 7 in the triangle to make a total of 12.

INVESTIGATION

Complete the following table.

Numbers used	0–5	1–6	2–7	3–8	4–9	5–10	6–11	7–12
First possible total	6	9	12	15				
Second possible total	9	12	15	18				

Level 2

1. Put the numbers 1 to 8 in this square
to make a total of 13 along each side.
(Four numbers have been already inserted.)

2. Put in the numbers 2 to 9 to total 16.

3. Put in the numbers 3 to 10 to total 19.

4. Put in the numbers 4 to 11 to total 22.

INVESTIGATION

Complete the following table.

Numbers used	1–8	2–9	3–10	4–11	5–12	6–13	7–14	8–15
Magic constant	13	16	19	22				

Level 3

Put the numbers 1 to 9 in this triangle to
total 20. The corner numbers have been
inserted for you.

INVESTIGATIONS

1.(a) What do you notice about the total of pairs of opposite numbers
in the middle of each side of the square see-side sums?

 (b) Why is this so?

TEACHING NOTES FOR SEE-SIDE SUMS

SOLUTIONS TO ACTIVITIES

Level 1

Solutions begin from a corner number.
1. 4   2   3   1   5   0
2. 1   5   3   4   2   6
3. 5   3   4   2   6   1
4. 2   6   4   5   3   7

Level 2

1. 6   3   4   8   1   7   5   2
2. 7   4   5   9   2   8   6   3
3. 8   5   6   10   3   9   7   4
4. 9   6   7   11   4   10   8   5

Level 3

1. 4   7   3   6   8   1   5   2   9

SOLUTIONS TO INVESTIGATIONS

Level 1

Children should be encouraged to continue the table for as long as possible by solving each individual triangle until they discover the pattern. Solutions can be generated by adding one to each of the numbers in a 'previous' solution.

Starting from one solution, the second solution can be generated by moving each of the numbers one place further round the triangle, keeping the same order.

Level 2

The numbers 3 to 10 are each one greater than the numbers 2 to 9. When arranged around the square, these make a total of three more along each side. The numbers 4 to 11 are each one greater than the numbers 3 to 10. When arranged around the square, these make a total of three more along each side, etc.

Level 3

1.(a) The total of each pair is always the same.
  (b) The total of each pair is the sum of the four corner numbers.

SHORTCUTS

INTRODUCTION

Here are some road maps. The time it takes to cycle down each road is given in minutes. Can you find the quickest route from *start* (S) to *home* (H)? For example, one route in the first map in Level 1 would take 3+7+1+3=14 minutes.

Level 1

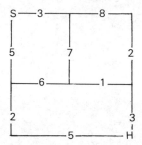
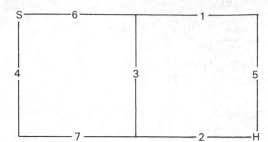

Level 2

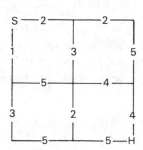
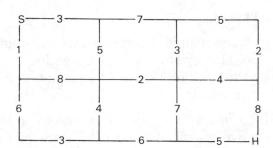

Level 3

Note You must not make a turn at crossroads without a circled number.

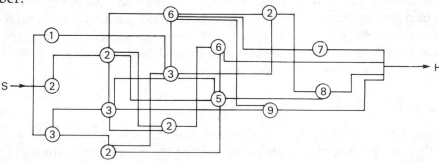

INVESTIGATIONS

Level 1

Investigate the number of possible ways of travelling from S to H in the diagram below.
For example,
J to K to N to S
J to M to P to S
J to M to R to U
L to O to P to S
etc.

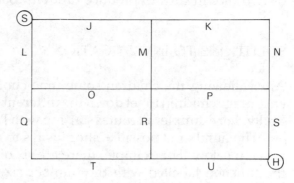

Level 2

Do the same with this diagram. Put in your own letters.

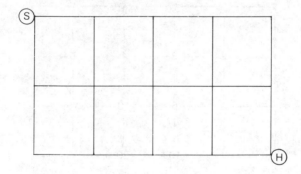

Level 3

Find all the different ways of travelling from S to H on this route map. What is the total number of minutes for each route?

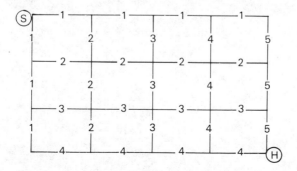

TEACHING NOTES FOR SHORTCUTS

Sheets of A4 paper can be duplicated or large-squared graph-paper can be used, containing various routes, with blanks for teachers or children to insert their own numbers. Children in pairs can throw one or two dice in turn to produce random road numbers.

SOLUTIONS TO INVESTIGATIONS

After allowing the children some time choosing routes at random, encourage children to set down the different possible routes systematically. For example, all routes starting with J, all routes starting J to H, etc. The number of possible 'short' ways to reach any given junction is given below. For example, there are six different ways of reaching the junction labelled with the number six. For those with a background in algebra, all these numbers are obtained from Pascal's Triangle.

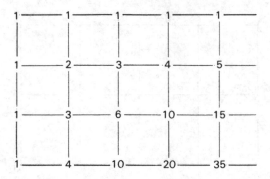

MAGIC SQUARES

INTRODUCTION

This is a magic square.
It contains the numbers 1, 2, 3, 4, 5, 6, 7, 8, 9.
Each row of the square adds up to 15,
e.g. 8+1+6=15. Each column adds up
to 15. Each diagonal adds up to 15.
15 is called the magic constant of the magic square.

8	1	6
3	5	7
4	9	2

ACTIVITIES

Level 1

1. This magic square uses only the numbers
2, 3, 4, 5, 6, 7, 8, 9, 10.
Each row, column and diagonal adds to 18.
So the magic constant is 18.
Fill in the missing numbers.

	2	7
4		
	10	

2. This magic square uses only the numbers
3, 4, 5, 6, 7, 8, 9, 10, 11.
The magic constant is 21.
Fill in the missing numbers.

10	3	
		9
	11	

3. Do the same with these magic squares.

(a) Use numbers 4 to 12.
Magic constant = 24.

11		
	12	

(b) Use numbers 5 to 13.
Magic constant = 27.

	9	

(c) Use numbers 6 to 14.
Magic constant = 30.

(d) Use numbers 7 to 15.
Magic constant = ?

4. Make your own magic square.
Numbers used . . .
Magic constant =

INVESTIGATION

Complete the following table:

Numbers used	1–9	2–10	3–11	4–12	5–13	6–14	7–15	8–16	9–17	10–18
Magic constant	15	18								

What do you notice?

Level 2

1. The numbers 1 to 16 can be used to make
a 4×4 magic square.
Its magic constant = 34.
Fill in the missing numbers.

16		2	13
	10	11	
9			12
	15		

2. Do the same with these magic squares.
(a) Use numbers
2 to 17.
M.C. = 38.

17			14
5			2

(b) Use numbers
3 to 18.
M.C. = 42.

(c) Use numbers
4 to 19.
M.C. = ?

INVESTIGATION

Complete the following table:

Numbers used	1–16	2–17	3–18	4–19	5–20	6–21	7–22	8–23
Magic constant	34	38						

What do you notice?

Level 3

1. This magic square uses only
some of the numbers up to 23.
Its M.C. = 41.
Can you fill in the missing numbers?

21		12	
	10		23
4			9

2. Can you find groups of four numbers in the square that also add to 41?

3. Can you find groups of four numbers in a 4×4 square with M.C. = 34 that add to 34?

INVESTIGATION

Can you complete this 5×5 magic square with M.C. = 65?

17	24			15
	5	7	14	
4			20	
10		19		3
		25	2	9

TEACHING NOTES FOR MAGIC SQUARES

SOLUTIONS TO ACTIVITIES

Level 1

Solutions (left to right, and row by row).
1.   9   2   7,   4   6   8,   5 10   3
2.   10   3   8,   5   7   9,   6 11   4
3.(a) 11   4   9,   6   8 10,   7 12   5
3.(b) 12   5 10,   7   9 11,   8 13   6
3.(c) 13   6 11,   8 10 12,   9 14   7
3.(d) 14   7 12,   9 11 13,   10 15   8

Level 2

1.   16   3   2 13,   5 10 11   8,   9   6   7 12,   4 15 14   1
2.(a) 17   4   3 14,   6 11 12   9,   10   7   8 13,   5 16 15   2
2.(b) 18   5   4 15,   7 12 13 10,   11   8   9 14,   6 17 16   3
2.(c) 19   6   5 16,   8 13 14 11,   12   9 10 15,   7 18 17   4

Level 3

1. 21   1   12   7,   11   8   20   2,   5   10   3   23,   4   22   6   9
2. The indicated groups of four numbers all total the magic constant.

X	X	O	O
X	X	O	O
O	O	X	X
O	O	X	X

O			O
	X	X	
	X	X	
O			O

	X	O	
X			O
O			X
	O	X	

	X	X	
O			O
O			O
	X	X	

3. The groups of numbers are in the same relative positions as for the previous question.

SOLUTIONS TO INVESTIGATIONS

Level 1

Since each of the three numbers in each row, column and diagonal increases by 1, the total for each row, column and diagonal increases by 3.

Level 2

Since each of the four numbers in each row, column and diagonal increases by 1, the total for each row, column and diagonal increases by 4.

Level 3

The 5×5 magic square is:

17	24	1	(8)	15
(23)	5	7	14	(16)
4	(6)	13	20	(22)
10	(12)	19	(21)	3
(11)	(18)	25	2	9

It is suggested that the numbers ringed are omitted if children are to find the solution by reasoning. Omit one other number if children are to use trial-and-error methods.

NOTE

It is possible to deduce the numbers in the initial 3×3 square without any clues as follows. To make a square total of 15, 5 must go in the middle and each pair of numbers on either side of the central 5 must total 10, i.e. 1+9, 2+8, 3+7, 4+6. If the 9 goes in a corner, then 8 must go in the middle of a side away from 9 and adjacent to the 1. But then 7 cannot be placed anywhere in the square (since we have no zero). Nine is therefore in the centre of a side and 8 in one of the two corners away from the 9. This forces the 7 into the centre of a side away from the 8 and 9. The remaining numbers are now determined.

Additional Notes

1. *To make any 3×3 magic square.* Begin with any number at the centre, say 20. The M.C. will be three times this number (60). Choose any other number for a corner. If this is greater than the centre number by y, then make the opposite corner number $20-y$ to compensate and make a total of 3×20. Choose any other number for another corner, say $20+z$. Compensate for this with a number $20-z$ in the opposite corner. The other numbers are determined by adding and subtracting y and z appropriately as shown to retain a total of 60.

$20+y$		$20+z$
	20	
$20-z$		$20-y$

$\longrightarrow$

$20+y$	$20-y-z$	$20+z$
$20-y+z$	20	$20-z+y$
$20-z$	$20+z+y$	$20-y$

If $y=10$ and $z=6$, this makes the magic square shown.

30	4	26
16	20	24
14	36	10

Divide by 2
M.C. = 60

15	2	13
8	10	12
7	18	5

M.C. = 30

Note. When creating new squares from the original 3×3 square, adding 1 to a number in each row and column adds 3 to the M.C.

2. *To make 4×4 magic squares.* Another series of magic squares can be made by adding (or subtracting) any number to the ringed numbers in the squares of the 4×4 square (i.e. a square in each row, column and diagonal).

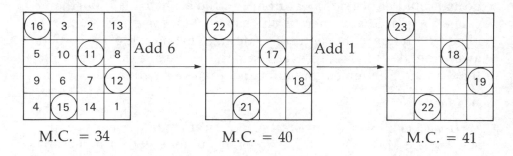

M.C. = 34   M.C. = 40   M.C. = 41

ACTIVITIES FOR MORE ABLE CHILDREN

1. Make the 4×4 magic square with M.C. = 41 without partial completion of the square.

2.(a) Find the M.C. of the 7×7 magic square shown that uses the numbers 1 to 49.

   (b) Now fill in the missing numbers.

		48		10	19	28
	47			9	18	27	29
46	6	8		26		37
5		16	25	34	36	
13	15	24	33	42		4
21	23		41		3	12
	31	40	49	2		

SOLUTIONS TO ACTIVITIES FOR MORE ABLE CHILDREN

1. See solution to Level 3, Activity 1.

2.(a) The M.C. is the sum of all the numbers used, divided by the number of rows. For example, for the 3×3 square, $1+2+3+ \ldots +9 = 45$. Divided by 3 this makes 15. For the 7×7 square, $1+2+3+4+5 + \ldots + 49$ is found by the formula $(1+n^2) \times n^2 \div 2$, where n is the number of rows. Each row therefore totals one nth of this.

When $n=7$, M.C. $= \dfrac{50\times49\div2}{7} = 175$.

(b) The 7×7 magic square is completed by adding the following numbers in the spaces—reading left to right and down—(missing numbers only): 30, 39, 1; 38, 37; 17, 35; 14, 45; 44; 32, 43; 22, 11, 20.

4-IN-A-LINE

INTRODUCTION

A game for two players with one calculator, using counters and a prepared board.

ACTIVITIES

Level 1: addition

Rules
1. Choose one number from the first rectangle and one number from the second rectangle.

9	17	19	27

6	11	15	24

2. Add the two numbers together on your calculator.
3. Find the number you obtain on the board and cover it with a counter.
4. The first player with a connected line of four numbers (horizontally, vertically or diagonally) is the winner.

23	33	28	34
25	15	38	33
43	32	30	42
24	51	41	20

Level 2: multiplication

Rules
Choose any two numbers from the small square and multiply them together on your calculator. Play as for Level 1, using the board shown.

6	1.9	40
0.4	0.9	0.5
1.5	14	2.5

0.2	0.6	1.25	26.6	2.4	1.35
12.6	84	16	560	36	2.85
1.71	240	7	1	35	5.6
11.4	20	3	9	100	5.4
0.95	76	21	15	60	0.45
3.75	2.25	0.75	4.75	0.76	0.36

Level 3: division

Rules

Choose any number above the line and divide it by any number below the line. Play as for Level 1 using the board shown.

0.4	1	2.4	4
0.6	12		16
2	5	0.8	0.5
10	0.25		0.2

6	0.48	80	24	1.2	15
2.4	0.75	0.4	0.06	0.8	9.6
16	0.04	2	3	0.5	64
48	0.3	5	4	0.24	20
3.2	0.1	0.08	0.2	0.12	4.8
12	1.25	32	60	1.6	8

MAKING THE MOST

INTRODUCTION

Arrange a given set of numbers in the boxes to make the answer to the sum as great as possible. For example, using the numbers 5, 6, 7 and multiplication:

```
    5  7                          6  7
  ×    6        is greater than  ×    5
  --------                        --------
  3  4  2                        3  3  5
  --------                        --------
```

ACTIVITIES

Level 1

Addition
1. Put the numbers 1, 2, 3, 4 in the boxes of this addition sum to make the answer as great as possible.

2. Put the numbers 1, 2, 3, 4, 5, 6 in the boxes of this addition sum to make the answer as great as possible.

Subtraction
3. Put the numbers 1, 2, 3, 4 in the boxes of this subtraction sum to make the answer:

(a) as great as possible;
(b) as small as possible.

Level 2

Multiplication
1. Put the numbers 3, 4, 5 in the boxes of this multiplication sum to make the answer as great as possible. Use your calculator to help you.

2. Put the numbers 2, 3, 4, 5 in the boxes of this multiplication sum to make the answer as great as possible. Use your calculator to help you.

3. Put the numbers 1, 2, 3, 4, 5 in the boxes of this multiplication sum to make the answer as great as possible. Use your calculator to help you.

Level 3

Use your calculator to make up other examples of your own.

TEACHING NOTES FOR MAKING THE MOST

SOLUTIONS TO ACTIVITIES

Level 1

1. $42 + 31 = 73$
2. $642 + 531 = 1,173$ or $542 + 631 = 1,173$, etc.
3. (a) $43 - 12 = 31$
   (b) $23 - 14 = 9$ or $41 - 32 = 9$

Level 2

1. $43 \times 5 = 215$
2. $432 \times 5 = 2,160$
3. $421 \times 53 = 22,313$

4
Developing reasoning

This book is concerned with mathematical and scientific thinking. Thinking is not an easy term to define. It has been perceptively described as an internal vision that we direct at experience in order to explore, understand and enlarge it—or more succinctly as 'the deliberate mental exploration of experience for a purpose' (De Bono, 1976, p. 30). The particular kind of thinking with which this chapter is concerned is that of reasoning.

The ability to reason forms an important thread linking children's mathematical and scientific thinking. Reasoning skills are becoming increasingly important in all areas of life, and the ability to evaluate a reasoned argument is assumed by many parts of the secondary school curriculum. Some of the aims of a mathematics scheme suggested in the Cockcroft Report include the ability to think and to reason logically, together with the ability to solve problems. Since this is a skill that is not specifically developed elsewhere on the school timetable, it seems important to include here activities relevant to this.

If we accept the importance of giving children practice in reasoning, is it necessary (or even possible) to teach it? For children who may be poorly motivated, abstract or generalised thinking does not come easily. The Cockcroft Committee recognised that the quality of mathematical thinking is often more important than the mathematics itself but offered little advice on how this type of thinking might be more systematically stimulated and developed.

A direct approach—teaching logic as a system of rules (implication, negation, etc.)—would be wholly unsuitable for less able or even 'average' children in primary school classes. Alternatively, providing teachers with a list of common errors that children make when arguing and discussing offers no motivation for children to improve their reasoning skills. Children need to have a purpose if they are to practise logical thinking; they should use it as a means to an end or, for example, as a necessary step to arriving at a solution to a problem they wish to solve.

An approach that is widely recommended by HMI and many other authorities in both mathematics and science is to use puzzles and games that embody these criteria of providing a purpose for children's thinking, although we should not underestimate the importance of an ability to solve puzzles as a skill in its own right. However, preparing suitable puzzles and games to match the abilities of all the children in a class is a difficult and time-consuming task for teachers and the purpose of this chapter is to present a number of such activities together with sufficient teaching notes to enable them to be used immediately by teachers without further preparation.

IDEAS TO START CHILDREN THINKING

How the following activities are used will depend both on the interests and abilities of the class and also on the teaching style of the teacher. Activities can be used as 'one-off' sessions or as part of a continuing theme. Some will be useful at the start or finish of a lesson while others might be made the culmination of a carefully prepared sequence of 'work' along the lines indicated.

It is possible to begin with the puzzle or game and then give guidance after the children have thought about it. Alternatively, a session can begin at a very simple level and gradually move up, step by step, to a more complex level. Although only one solution to a problem may be given in the text, other valid answers and approaches offered by children should be welcomed. A special feature of these activities is the extensive teaching notes accompanying most puzzles or investigations. The activities have been divided into three stages or levels of difficulty in order to maximise the adaptability of the activity to different levels of understanding. Extension activities or further problems for more able children have been suggested where appropriate. The activities have been grouped for the convenience of teachers in planning as follows:

Logical thinking

- Minibeasts
- Children's choice
- Brain games

Spatial reasoning

- Pentominoes
- Polyominoes
- Squares within squares

Puzzle solving

- Chessboard queens
- Puzzles to pour over
- Tower of Hanoi

Games of strategy

- Mistermind
- Mini-chess
- Crosses and noughts

Imaginative thinking

- About numbers
- About situations
- About language

LOGICAL THINKING

The activities in this section have been loosely grouped under the category of 'logical thinking'. What is logical thinking? Is it anything more than thinking that is not illogical? The usual primary school approach to teaching logic has been through sorting, ordering and matching activities that lead to the topic of 'sets'. However, activities that require discrimination between different attributes of triangles, circles and squares have a limited interest to children as they grow older. Other approaches through 'lateral thinking' have been tried successfully (De Bono, 1972) but require some training and commitment on the part of the teacher in order to carry them out effectively, HMI (DES, 1979) suggest that logic in the primary school should consist of the following.

- Noting resemblances and differences.
- Describing things accurately.
- Saying how things are related.
- Finding the best moves in games and puzzles.

The aim of the activities presented here is to provide an alternative to traditional classroom approaches to logic. This selection of logical puzzles is offered in the hope that children will enjoy the experience, perhaps new to some children, of 'thinking logically'.

Activities are as follows.

- Minibeasts
- Children's choice
- Brain games

MINIBEASTS

INTRODUCTION

Sara collects mice, beetles and snakes and she loves counting. She always likes to count the number of legs and heads of the little animals in her collection!

ACTIVITIES

Level 1

Sara has 1 beetle and 1 mouse

1. How many legs is that? (Beetles have 6 legs.)

2. Her mouse escapes but her friend gives her 3 snakes instead. How many heads does she have now?

3. She now swops some of her pets so that she has 2 beetles, 3 mice and 1 snake. How many legs is that altogether?

Level 2

1. One week when she counts up she finds she has 3 heads and 10 legs. Which pets must she have now?

2. She counts them again later and finds she now has 4 heads and 10 legs. Which pets must she have?

3. If she has 3 heads and 8 legs, which pets does she have?

4. If she has 3 heads and 12 legs, which pets does she have? Are you sure of your answer?

Level 3

1. 34 legs and 9 heads. How many pets is that?

2. 26 legs and 12 heads. How many pets is that?

3. Make up your own problems with lorries (6 wheels), cars (4 wheels) and 3-wheeler bikes.

TEACHING NOTES FOR MINIBEASTS

SOLUTIONS TO ACTIVITIES

Level 2

1. 1 beetle, 1 mouse, 1 snake.
2. 1 beetle, 1 mouse, 2 snakes.
3. 2 mice, 1 snake.
4. 2 beetles, 1 snake *or* 3 mice.

Level 3

1. 3 beetles, 4 mice, 2 snakes *or* 5 beetles, 1 mouse, 3 snakes *or* 1 beetle, 7 mice, 1 snake.
2. 3 beetles, 2 mice, 7 snakes *or* 1 beetle, 5 mice, 6 snakes.

Note
There may be more than one solution to a question and tables may be drawn up to find these. For example,

Beetles	0	0	0	1	1	1	1	2	2	2	2	3	3	3	3
Mice	1	2	3	0	1	2	3	0	1	2	3	0	1	2	3
Total number of legs	4	8	12	6	10	14	18	12	16	20	24	18	22	26	30

Similar problems can be invented with numbers of octopus (8 legs) and starfish (5 legs).

CHILDREN'S CHOICE

INTRODUCTION

Four friends, Andy, Bob, Cathy and Debbie, went down to the beach and hired four beach cabins—numbered 11, 12, 13, 14—next to each other. After their swim, they forgot whose cabin was whose. Bob remembered that his cabin had an even number and Debbie remembered that she was not next to Bob. Andy said he was definitely not next to Cathy or Debbie.

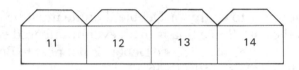

ACTIVITIES

Level 1

Where did the children finally find their clothes? *Additional clue* Cathy remembered she was in cabin 13.

Level 2

Where did the children finally find their clothes? No additional clue.

Level 3

The same four children want to buy one pet each: a rabbit, a dog, a cat and a duck. Their four gardens are next to each other in the order Andy, Bob, Cathy, Debbie, but only Bob and Debbie have ponds for the duck. They decide that the dog cannot go next door to the duck and the rabbit cannot go next door to either the cat or the dog.

Who buys which pets?

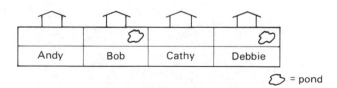

= pond

TEACHING NOTES FOR CHILDREN'S CHOICE

Less able children should begin at Level 1. More able children should not be given the Level 1 clue. The two problems (Levels 1 and 2, and Level 3) are essentially identical, and use the same logical strategy. The simple logical strategy used in these examples should be explained several times to children if they are to acquire a 'feel' for true logical reasoning.

SOLUTIONS TO ACTIVITIES

Level 2

If Andy is not next to Cathy or Debbie then he must be next to Bob and in an end cabin. Since Bob is in an even-numbered cabin, Andy must be in 11 and Bob in 12. Since Debbie is not next to Bob she must be in 14 and therefore Cathy is in 13.

Andy	Bob	Cathy	Debbie
11	12	13	14

Level 3

One solution strategy is to begin by considering the placing of the duck. If the duck is Debbie's, then the rabbit cannot be put in any of the remaining three positions (since it cannot go next to the dog or the cat). Therefore the duck must go to Bob. The rabbit, which must be kept away from the dog and the cat, must go to Andy. Therefore the dog must go to Debbie, to be kept away from the duck. So Cathy has the cat.

rabbit	duck	cat	dog
Andy	Bob	Cathy	Debbie

BRAIN GAMES

INTRODUCTION

None of these logical exercises is easy. The negatively worded expression is particularly difficult for children to handle and a considerable degree of practice is required before children are able to draw what may appear to be an obvious conclusion.

For example, consider the following: 'Bill is not older than Tom. Is Tom older than Bill?' This is not an easy question for many children to answer and plenty of time should be given to enable children to think through for themselves the implications of such statements.

The two examples given below should be worked through patiently on the blackboard and as much time as required allowed to all the children.

Example 1

The fathers of Nicky and Lisa are called Mr Jones and Mr Brown. Mr Brown is older than Mr Jones. Nicky's father is not younger than Lisa's father. Who is Lisa's father?

Solution strategy to suggest to the children
Is Nicky's father younger than Lisa's?—No.
Therefore is Nicky's father older than Lisa's?—Yes.
Who is the older father?—Mr Brown.
So who is Nicky's father?—Mr Brown.
Therefore who is Lisa's father?—Mr Jones.

Example 2

On a school trip there are three girls and three boys. The girls are Debbie, Sara and Julie. The boys are Rob, Jim and Graham, The girls are told to make partners with the boys. Use the following clues to find whose partner was whose.

Clues
1. Jim is older than Graham.
2. Julie's partner is younger than Graham.
3. Debbie is not Rob's partner.
4. Sara's partner is not the oldest.

Solution strategy to suggest to children
   Look at the ages Jim is older than Graham, so Jim is not youngest. Julie's partner is younger than Graham, so Graham is not youngest. So Rob is youngest (and Jim is oldest).
   Look at partners Julie's partner is youngest, so it is Rob. Sara's partner is not the oldest so it must be Graham. Therefore Debbie's partner is Jim.
   A table is helpful.

Girl	Girl's partner	Not girl's partner
Debbie		
Sara		
Julie		

ACTIVITIES

Level 1

Three famous scientists had the first names Isaac, Benjamin and Auguste. Their surnames were Franklin, Newton and Piccard. They were born in France, England and America. Find their surnames and the countries in which they were born. Use these clues:

1. Isaac's surname was Newton.
2. Auguste didn't live in England.
3. Benjamin lived in America.
4. Benjamin's surname was not Piccard.

Make a table.

Scientist	Surname	Country
Isaac		
Auguste		
Benjamin		

Level 2

Three teachers work at a school—Miss White, Mrs Green and Mr Black. Their christian name initials are K, N and T. They have taught at the school for 4 years, 9 years and 11 years. For each teacher, find the number of years they have taught and their initials. Use these clues:

1. Miss White has taught for 7 years longer than the teacher with initial K.
2. Mr Black, whose initial is not T, has been at the school for 9 years.

Make a table.

Teacher	Initial	Years teaching
Miss White		
Mrs Green		
Mr Black		

Level 3

Four Americans—Amy, Bob, Chris and Darth—have four pen-friends. The pen-friends have the names Juma, Yusuf, Nadir and Jean. They live in England, India, France and Kenya, and their ages are 8, 9, 10 and 11 years. Find the details of each American's pen-friend. Use these clues:

1. Amy's European pen-friend is the youngest.
2. Bob's English pen-friend is older than both Darth's and Chris's pen-friends.
3. Juma comes from Kenya and Nadir is not English.
4. Chris's Indian pen-friend is younger than Juma.
5. Jean is the youngest pen-friend.

Make a table.

American	Pen-friend	Pen-friend's age	Pen-friend's country
Amy			
Bob			
Chris			
Darth			

TEACHING NOTES FOR BRAIN GAMES

SOLUTIONS TO ACTIVITIES

Level 1

Isaac Newton—England.
Auguste Piccard—France.
Benjamin Franklin—America.

Level 2

Miss T White—11 years.
Mrs K Green—4 years.
Mr N Black—9 years.

Level 3

Bob's pen-friend is English, so Amy's European pen-friend is French (clue 1). So Darth's pen-friend is Kenyan—since Chris's is Indian (clue 4). Bob's pen-friend is older than Darth's and Chris's (clue 2) and Amy's is not the oldest (clue 1), so Bob's is oldest (i.e. 11 years). Amy's is therefore youngest—i.e. 8 years (clue 1). Therefore Amy's pen-friend is Jean (clue 5). Nadir is not English (clue 3) so Nadir is Indian. Therefore Yusuf is English.

SPATIAL REASONING

The activities collected here involve spatial reasoning and intuition. Exploring shape, pattern, symmetry and tessellation (the fitting together of shapes to leave no spaces in between) is an important part of children's mathematical development. In a recent publication, HMI (DES, 1985) advocate that mathematics for all pupils, including low attainers, should contain a considerable geometrical component. They stress that work should be undertaken in both two and three dimensions with the aim of developing children's spatial thinking. As an example of an activity through which may be developed general strategies and problem-solving, the Cockcroft Report (para. 323) suggests the activity of counting the number of lines joining up different numbers of points lying on a circle. Similar activities have been suggested in this section.

Any enjoyable mathematical activity will develop a positive attitude to the subject and these few suggestions are offered with at least this minimal aim. Activities are as follows.

- Pentominoes
- Polyominoes
- Squares within squares

PENTOMINOES

INTRODUCTION

Pentominoes are formed when five squares are joined together along their edges in different ways. The shapes can be cut out of squared paper and stuck onto cardboard if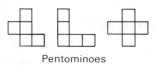

Pentominoes

preferred but interlocking cubes are a more suitable medium for young children. The protrusions can be cut off cubes such as Multi-link or Osmiroid once these have been formed into pentominoes.

ACTIVITIES

Level 1

1. Make all possible pentomino shapes with cubes or by drawing on squared paper.

2. Fit the shapes made into a 10 × 6 rectangular 'jigsaw' and colour them in if drawn on paper. Learn how to solve the jigsaw puzzle without referring to the solution.

3. Find out which of the shapes can be turned over and fitted back into the jigsaw.

Level 2

1. *Pentomino game* Two players take turns to place one of the set of twelve pentominoes onto a chessboard (8 × 8). The last player able to fit a shape onto the board is the winner.

2. Find out which pentominoes will tessellate (completely fill an area).

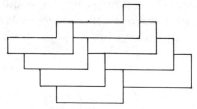

Tessellating pentominoes

3. Fit the twelve pentominoes onto the following sizes of rectangular boards: 5 × 12 units, 4 × 15 units, 3 × 20 units (each pentomino square is considered to be one unit long).

Level 3

1. A large pentomino shape can be made as shown.

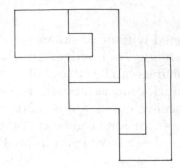

Make the following larger pentomino shapes with smaller pentomino shapes. Each shape should be twice as long and twice as wide as the smaller pentomino (therefore each shape will require four small pentominoes).

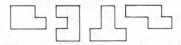

2. Use *all* the pentomino shapes to fill a chessboard apart from the central four squares.

TEACHING NOTES FOR PENTOMINOES

SOLUTIONS TO ACTIVITIES

Level 1

2. There are twelve possible shapes that fit together (there are many alternative solutions).

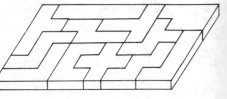

3. The following shapes can be turned completely over and fitted back into the jigsaw. They are therefore symmetrical shapes.

Level 2

2. The following shapes and others will tessellate.

3. The figures shown are just one way of arranging the pentominoes into rectangles.

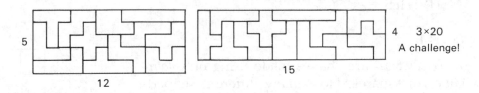

4   3×20
A challenge!

Level 3

1. If necessary, children can be given the four pentominoes required to make each shape.

2.

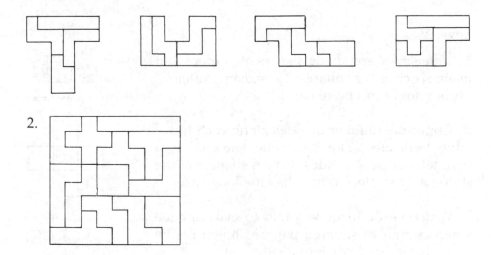

POLYOMINOES

INTRODUCTION

These are activities that are ideally carried out with interlocking cubes. However, squared paper and a pencil are often a convenient substitute.

ACTIVITIES

Level 1

1. *Tetrominoes* are shapes made using only *four* cubes or squares. How many different shaped tetrominoes can you make?

A tetromino

2. *Tetraboloes* are made from four *triangles* joined along their sides. How many of the fourteen different tetraboloes can you make?

A tetrabolo

Level 2

1. *Hexominoes* are made like pentominoes but using *six* cubes or squares. How many different hexominoes can you make?

A hexomino

2. Count the number of sides along each hexomino perimeter. The hexomino shown has a perimeter of twelve sides. Which shape has the shortest perimeter? Which has the longest?

3. Which hexominoes will fold to make a cube when cut out of squared paper? Shown is one such shape that folds into a cube.

Level 3

1. *Heptominoes* are made using *seven* cubes or squares. How many of the 108 different heptominoes can you make in fifteen minutes? (Allow the children to work on this problem in their own time if sufficient interest is shown.)

2. *Octominoes* are made using *eight* cubes or squares. How many of the 369 different octominoes can you find which are symmetrical about a line? (In other words, which will fit back into a jigsaw when turned over?) Shown is an octomino with two lines of symmetry.

TEACHING NOTES FOR POLYOMINOES

SOLUTIONS TO ACTIVITIES

Level 1

1. The five possible tetrominoes.

2. Fourteen tetraboloes.

Level 2

1. There are 35 possible hexominoes.

2. The shortest perimeter is 10 sides long.

The longest perimeter is 14 sides long.

3. Eleven hexominoes will fold to make cubes. Here are the other ten.

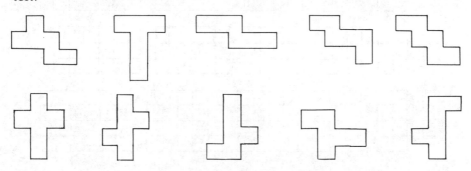

SQUARES WITHIN SQUARES

INTRODUCTION

Count how many squares are here altogether.

There are four small squares and one large square.
We can show the answer like this.

ACTIVITIES

Level 1

How many squares altogether in these figures? Write your answers in the correct sized squares.

Level 2

How many squares altogether in these figures?

a   b   c   d   e   f

1.

2.

3.

Level 3

How many squares in these *squares?*

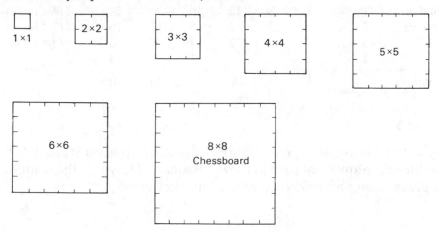

TEACHING NOTES FOR SQUARES WITHIN SQUARES

Let the children discover the patterns for themselves in Levels 2 and 3.

SOLUTIONS TO ACTIVITIES

Level 1

(a) 8   (b) 11   (c) 14   (d) 12   (e) 14   (f) 17

Level 2

		a	b	c	d	e	f
		Number of squares in each rectangular figure					
Size of	1×1	2	4	6	8	10	12
square	2×2		1	2	3	4	5
Total no.		2	5	8	11	14	17

		a	b	c	d	e	f
		Number of squares in each rectangular figure					
Size of	1×1	3	6	9	12	15	18
square	2×2		2	4	6	8	10
	3×3			1	2	3	4
Total no.		3	8	14	20	26	32

		Number of squares in each rectangular figure						
		a	b	c	d	e	f	
Size of	1×1	4	8	12	16	20	24	... (4× table)
square	2×2		3	6	9	12	15	... (3× table)
	3×3			2	4	6	8	... (2× table)
	4×4				1	2	3	
Total no.		4	11	20	30	40	50	

Level 3

By noting the possible positions for each size of square it is possible to deduce the number of each in the 8 × 8 square. However the solution is given below by reference to the table patterns.

		Number of squares in each rectangular figure							
		a	b	c	d	e	f	g	h
Size of	1×1	1	4	9	16	25	36	49	64
square	2×2		1	4	9	16	25	36	49
	3×3			1	4	9	16	25	36
	4×4				1	4	9	16	25
	5×5					1	4	9	16
	6×6						1	4	9
	7×7							1	4
	8×8								1
Total no.		1	5	14	30	55	91	140	204

PUZZLE SOLVING

Puzzles have been regarded in the past as merely recreational diversions that had no relevance to the central issues of mathematical education. However, Cockcroft (para. 227) stated that puzzles and games can clarify the ideas in a syllabus and assist the development of logical thinking. For most puzzles, a general strategy may not be discoverable. The solution may depend on insight with a certain element of randomness. However, some sort of systematic and exhaustive trying out of all possibilities is usually more successful. Some puzzles have more of the character of 'tricks', which once learned can be performed without any mental effort. Tricks are always popular with children and if initially acquiring the solution to a trick involves a mathematical or geometrical principle, then this principle will be used and possibly recalled each time the trick is carried out.

In puzzles, children meet a task that is seemingly impossible, but that nevertheless does have a solution—one that may render the puzzle absurdly easy or obvious when discovered. When watching an adult trying to solve a puzzle to which they know the answer, children will see the same reactions of frustration which *they* first experienced and will derive great satisfaction and a boost to self-confidence in subsequently explaining the solution. Activities are as follows.

- Chessboard queens
- Puzzles to pour over
- Tower of Hanoi

CHESSBOARD QUEENS (NO TWO IN A LINE)

INTRODUCTION

These puzzles involve placing the maximum number of counters onto a squared board (one counter per square) such that no two counters are in line either horizontally, vertically or diagonally. The problem is equivalent to placing chess queens onto a chessboard so that no two can 'take' each other.

ACTIVITIES

Level 1

1. Place two counters in the above way onto a 3 × 3 square.
2. Place four counters onto a 4 × 4 square.
3. Place five counters onto a 5 × 5 square.

Level 2

1. Place six counters onto a 6 × 6 square.
2. Place seven counters onto a 7 × 7 square.

Level 3

Place eight counters onto an 8 × 8 square. This is the classic 'eight queens on a chessboard' problem.

TEACHING NOTES FOR CHESSBOARD QUEENS

SOLUTIONS TO ACTIVITIES

(These are not the only solutions.)

Level 1

Level 2

Solutions refer to an alphabetical/numerical square matrix. Thus A1 is a corner square, etc.

1. D1, A2, E3, B4, F5, C6.
2. D1, A2, E3, B4, F5, C6, G7.

Level 3

F1, D2, G3, A4, H5, B6, E7, C8.

Note

There is a pattern to the solutions for the 4×4 to 7×7 boards that can be used by the children but this breaks down for the full 8×8 chessboard. The chessboard solution is, however, rotationally symmetrical about a diagonal of the square and the queens in each half of the board are related by a chessboard 'knight's path'. Further investigation of the effect of the 'knight's path' can be carried out for larger boards, although the pattern is complex.

PUZZLES TO POUR OVER

ACTIVITIES

Level 1

Can you pour out half a glass of water using only an empty glass and one of the same size known to be three-quarters full?

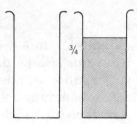

Level 2

1. Can you pour out 1 litre of water using only 5-litre and 2-litre jars?

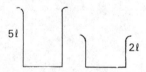

2. Given the following six jars (a), three full and three empty in the order shown, can you make the row of six jars alternate with full and empty jars as shown (b)—but by moving only one of the glasses?

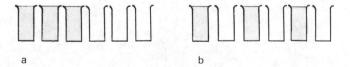

a   b

Level 3

1. Can you pour out 4 litres using only 5-litre and 3-litre jars?

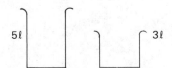

TEACHING NOTES TO PUZZLES TO POUR OVER

SOLUTIONS TO ACTIVITIES

Level 1

Make a mark one-quarter way up the empty glass using the top-quarter section of the three-quarters full glass. Now pour the water into the empty glass up to the mark made. Half a glass of water will now remain in the glass.

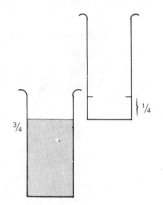

Level 2

1.

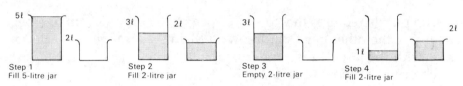

Now only 1 litre remains in the 5-litre jar.

2. Pour the liquid from the second glass into the fifth glass and replace it.

Level 3

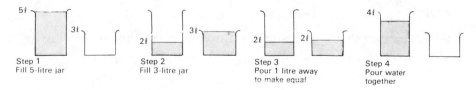

TOWER OF HANOI

INTRODUCTION

This well-known puzzle consists of a set of eight discs of increasing sizes that can be moved to any of three positions or placed on pegs. The usual form of the puzzle is a set of discs with holes in the centre that can be placed on three pegs set in a line.

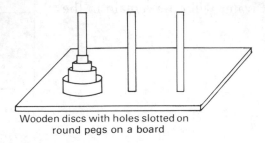

Wooden discs with holes slotted on
round pegs on a board

   The puzzle requires the 'tower' of pegs to be moved from one peg to any of the other pegs starting with the discs arranged in order of size with the largest disc underneath.
   The rules of moving are:

1. Only one disc at a time may be moved.
2. A larger disc may not be placed over a smaller one.

   Alternative forms of the game can simply be made from coins or thick cardboard discs placed on three clearly-marked positions on a board.

ACTIVITIES

Level 1

Use only three discs. Transfer the 'tower' to another peg following the rules above. The minimum number of moves required is seven.

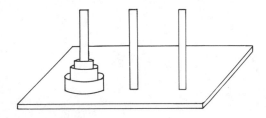

Level 2

Use only four discs. To transfer the tower requires a minimum of fifteen moves.

Level 3

Use five or more discs. Five discs takes 31 moves, six discs takes 63 moves. Seven discs takes 127 moves (see teaching notes).

TEACHING NOTES FOR TOWER OF HANOI

SOLUTIONS TO ACTIVITIES

Level 1

Use a triangular-shaped board with pegs in positions 1, 2, 3 in clockwise order as shown.

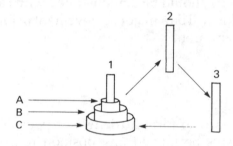

Let the smallest disc be A, the middle disc B and the largest disc C. The solution is:

A to 2, B to 3, A to 3, C to 2, A to 1, B to 2, A to 2.

Level 2

Let smallest disc be A and largest disc D. The solution is:

A to 2, B to 3, A to 3, C to 2, A to 1, B to 2, A to 2.

This takes the top three discs onto peg 2.

Then move D to 3, A to 3, B to 1, A to 1, C to 3, A to 2, B to 3, A to 3.

This takes the top three discs onto disc D on peg 3.

Level 3

The number of moves required for greater numbers of discs is $2^d - 1$, where d = the number of discs used. So,

$d = 5$ requires $2^5 - 1$ moves (= 31 moves).
$d = 6$ requires $2^6 - 1$ moves (= 63 moves).
$d = 8$ requires $2^8 - 1$ moves (= 255 moves), etc.

SOLUTION

The solution strategy should be shown to the children only after they have spent some time struggling with the problem. The appropriate time to introduce the solution will vary according to circumstances· but learning how to carry out the strategy is of equal if not more importance than the time spent trying to solve the problems since discovery of solutions beyond Level 1 will be beyond most less able children. Knowing *how* to solve the puzzles will give the children much confidence in demonstrating their skill and knowledge to adults. The strategy should be demonstrated with care and patience, since if learned this will be a major achievement in logical thinking for slower learning children.

Solution strategy

Move peg 2 forward to form a triangle of pegs. The smallest disc should now always be moved one position round in a clockwise direction on *every other turn*. On the other (alternate) turns, make the only other move possible—that is, move the smaller disc onto a larger disc.

GAMES OF STRATEGY

Cockcroft (para. 226) stated that maths should be a subject both to use and to enjoy. Games undoubtedly promote the latter and generate enthusiasm, excitement and involvement. They bring variety into a maths lesson and promote co-operation, perseverance and patience in the players—qualities often lacking in children with emotionally-linked learning difficulties. Games can also be a great help in the organisation of a class in which one or two children have learning needs that differ greatly from the rest of the class.

There are many games that can also be used to reinforce skills in number and other areas of mathematics. However, those selected here have not been chosen for this. The games in this section require some forethought in the choice or development of a strategy. Children must make a decision: if . . . then . . . what will happen? They must first make a conjecture and then try out or test that conjecture. In this way they learn by trial and (often) error.

Although some games teach themselves, others will repay the teacher's more careful consideration and familiarisation with the rules. The ideal way to do this is by playing the game with several of those children who are most likely to benefit from a systematic introduction. The rules of most games are best 'explained' by beginning a practice game and considering each rule as the necessity arises. The teacher's participation is invariably appreciated by the class and time spent in this way is most important if a game is to be successfully played and enjoyed. Activities are as follows.

- Mistermind
- Mini-chess
- Crosses and noughts

MISTERMIND

INTRODUCTION

This is a game for two players. The materials required are coloured counters. The aim is for one player to discover the order of coloured counters arranged by the other player.

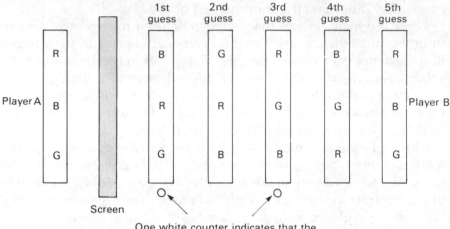

One white counter indicates that the
position of one coloured counter is correct

Play
1. Player A arranges three coloured counters (left to right) in an order that B cannot see.
2. Player B arranges his or her three counters in the order he or she thinks A has arranged them (first guess).
3. Player A indicates to B how many of B's counters are in correct positions by means of a white counter.
4. Player B leaves his or her first arrangement on display and uses three more counters to show his or her second guess.
5. Player A indicates to B again how many of B's counters are in correct positions.
6. Play continues until B has the correct order.

ACTIVITIES

Level 1

Have two counters of the same colour—say red (R), blue (B) and blue (B). There are only three arrangements possible: BRB, BBR and RBB.

This means the first and second attempts by player B are merely guesses and the third attempt is therefore obvious. This, however, is essential preparation for Level 2. Children should take the roles of both players before moving to Level 2.

Level 2

Use three different colours—say red (R), blue (B) and green (G). There are six possible arrangements BGR, BRG, GBR, GRB, RGB and RBG. Player A should indicate the result of each guess of player B by placing one white counter beside each arrangement that has one counter in the correct order but no white counter beside arrangements that have no counters in the correct order. From the absence or otherwise of these white counters, player B can deduce a correct arrangement sooner than by chance.

Level 3

Use four different coloured counters. It is essential that the results of each guess are recorded using a number of white counters to correspond to the number of counters in the correct places. (This is a similar game to the commercially popular *Mastermind*, which, however, uses six coloured counters.)

MINI-CHESS

INTRODUCTION

The following games were originally designed to be used as preparations for the full game of chess but have subsequently proved to be interesting games in their own right. Each game uses only some of the full set of chess pieces. The following instructions assume the teacher is already familiar with the rules of chess.

ACTIVITIES

Level 1

1. Pawn battles
All the pawns are arranged as for a normal game of chess. No other pieces are placed on the board and the pawns can move exactly as in the full game. The last player who is able to move is the winner.

2. King of the castles
Each player has only his king with two castles. Pieces move as in the full game. The aim is to 'take' the opponent's king. Kings start on white 'centre' squares and queen's side castles are moved one square in to avoid immediate confrontation.

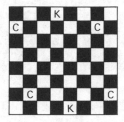

Level 2

1. Queens and bishops
Each player has only a queen and two bishops. Starting positions for the pieces are as in the full game with black queen moved to her adjacent white square. The aim is to take all of the opposing pieces.

2. Castles and pawns
A combination of pawn battles and king of the castles, with the castles and pawns (soldiers) protecting the king, who must not be taken.

Level 3

1. Knights of the square table
Only knights and pawns are used. Starting positions as in the full game. The aim is to take the opposing knights. (Knights are 'horses' that can jump over other pieces.)

2. Kings, castles, pawns and knights
The usual game of chess without queens and bishops.

3. The full game with the aim of 'taking' the king rather than forcing a checkmate.

CROSSES AND NOUGHTS

ACTIVITIES

Level 1: noughts and crosses

The playing strategies of this game are not always understood by children and the game provides a simple introduction to the more sophisticated games in Levels 2 and 3.

Two simple non-losing strategies can be practised by the children. These are:

1. First player wins if he or she starts on a corner or in the centre *and* the second player avoids the centre with his or her first move (as shown, where X has started and X can win).

2. There is a non-losing strategy for the second player provided he or she positions his or her first move in the centre or a corner (as shown, where X has started but O can avoid losing).

Level 2: trihex

This is a game for two players played on the board shown. Each player has his or her own coloured set of five counters. Players take turns to place one of their counters on the intersection of lines shown. The first player to make an unbroken line of three counters with his or her own colour wins. The game involves mainly blocking strategies but there are opportunities to win by thoughtful placing of counters in the central three intersections by the first player.

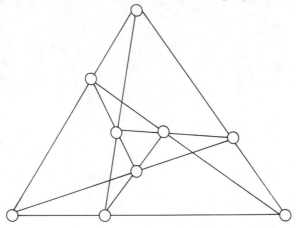

Level 3: no three in a line

A game for two players each with a set of coloured counters.

1. Begin with a 4 × 4 squared board. Players take turns to add a counter of their colour to the board, *avoiding* putting three in a line (horizontally, vertically or diagonally), whether adjacent or with empty squares in between. In the example shown, X began play and is here forced to lose on his or her next move.

	O		O
X		X	
O	O	X	O
	X		X

2. Use boards with a larger number of squares eventually progressing to a chessboard (8 × 8 square).

IMAGINATIVE THINKING

The foregoing sections involve constructive mathematical or scientific thinking requiring consistent and methodical strategies to be employed. Such structured thinking does not come easily to most primary aged children, particularly lower attaining children—hence the need for a book such as this. However, in certain situations, an ability to think outside of the conventional 'logical' framework can be an advantage. Sometimes the mind needs to resist a tendency to consider information only in its most conventional setting and to look in the *least* likely direction. Certain cues can create a strong and dominant pattern of thought that prevents the mind from considering other possibilities. For this reason, children can often solve a certain type of problem more quickly than adults, *particularly* if that adult happens to be a scientist, mathematician or teacher!

Perhaps some educationists will consider the inclusion of these 'problems' to be trivial in a book on mathematical and scientific thinking. They are included here because they are questions that require an answer and they involve thinking around numbers, situations or language. No strategies can be suggested since most 'solutions' are unique and specific to the question. Most require very special attention to the wording—a most important prerequisite to all problem-solving whether mathematical, scientific or other.

Most are not original and some have been adapted from or inspired by Martin Gardner's 'Thirty-seven Catch Questions' (in Gardner, 1969). A too literal interpretation of the questions is not in the spirit of the exercise. Pedants don't read on!

IMAGINATIVE THINKING—ABOUT NUMBERS

1.　The day before yesterday I was 10, but next year I'll be 13. How can this be?

2.　'How much is it for one?' Jane asked.
　'20p', the shopkeeper replied.
　'And how much is it for ten?'
　'Just 40p', was the answer.
　'OK, I'll take a hundred and ten', decided Jane.
　'That'll be 60p', said the shopkeeper.
What was Jane buying?

3.　A triangle has sides of 9 metres, 17 metres and 8 metres. What is its area?

4.　Make 101010 into nine-fifty by adding one line.

5.　If it takes 2½ minutes to cook one chestnut, how long would it take to cook three chestnuts?

6.　A science teacher bought 24 small magnets, gave half to her class and half of the remainder to her son—who lost all of them but four. How many had her son then left to play with?

7.　'How much is that bar of chocolate?' said Steve to Mr Ecks, who was looking after the school tuckshop.
　'5p plus half what it costs', said Mr Ecks.
How much did it cost?

8.　Two girls were born on the same day of the same month in the same year of the same parents—but they were not twins. Explain!

9.　Two Australian surf-boarders were jogging along Bondi beach. The older one claimed he was the father of the other one's son. How was this possible?

SOLUTIONS

1.　My birthday was yesterday—December 31st.
2.　Door numbers.

3. Zero square metres (you cannot draw a triangle with sides of these lengths).
4. 10 TO 10 (the time 9.50).
5. 2½ minutes.
6. Four magnets.
7. 10p.
8. They were two sisters of triplets.
9. They were husband and wife.

IMAGINATIVE THINKING—ABOUT SITUATIONS

1. *The slow race*

There was once a greedy king who didn't like giving his money away—not even to his own two sons. When the two sons were old enough to receive their inheritance, the king called them both to him and said, 'I intend to leave all my inheritance to only one of you and you must not share it between you. To decide which of you it will be, listen carefully to what you must do. You must each take your best horse and, starting together, ride right around the lake on my estate. I will give all my treasure to the son whose horse arrives *last*.'

The sons set off very slowly together, each making sure the other was not trailing behind. About half-way round, the first son said, 'This is silly and our father is very clever. As we approach nearer the house we will ride slower and slower and so eventually neither of us will ever get there to claim the inheritance. Our father knew that neither of us would ever come home again.'

They dismounted from their horses and sat down to think about what to do. Suddenly the second son had an idea and immediately told the first son about it. Then they both jumped up in a flash and rode off furiously towards home.

What was the second son's idea?

2. *Biggs' dilemma*

A bank robber in Brazil is escaping from the police with two 5-kilogram bags of money. He reaches a rope bridge that will *just* hold 8 kilograms more than his weight. The river is too wide to throw one of his bags across. How can he cross the bridge to escape with the money?

3. Kidnappers are holding a man hostage on their boat which is moored in the docks. They tie him to a steel ladder hanging over the side of the boat with his head one metre above the water. The tide is rising at three metres every hour. How long will it take before the water reaches his head and he drowns?

4. A man is found dead in the desert. Beside him is a large bag. If only he had opened the bag he wouldn't have died. What was in the bag?

5. Tom and Bill are coalmen. While they were delivering coal, I saw Tom carrying with great difficulty a single bag of coal to a house while

Bill was carrying three bags and almost running, without appearing to notice the weight. Why was this?

6. Which weighs more? One kilo of steel alloy ball-bearings or one kilo of glass marbles of exactly the same size as the steel alloy balls?

SOLUTIONS

1. To change horses.
2. By juggling with his two bags of money.
3. Never—the boat rises with the tide!
4. A parachute.
5. Tom's bag was full. Bill's bags were empty.
6. Neither—they both weigh one kilo.

IMAGINATIVE THINKING—ABOUT LANGUAGE

1. What is the exact opposite of 'not in'?

2. Re-arrange the letters of DROWN THE OAR to make another word.

3. Cross out six letters from SAIFXRLEUTITERTS to leave a fruit.

4. There is three mistakes in this sentense.
What are they?

SOLUTIONS

1. 'in'.
2. ANOTHER WORD.
3. A F R U I T (delete the words SIX LETTERS).
4.(a) 'is' should be 'are'.
   (b) Spelling of *sentence*.
   (c) There are (now) only *two* mistakes in the sentence!

5
Stimulating scientific thinking

It is stated at the outset of this book that the single most important factor in less able children's learning of science is the extent of their involvement and interest. This chapter is about some of the ways in which teachers can stimulate this interest across a wide range of scientific topics.

It should not be assumed that the interests of less able children are necessarily different from those of others and therefore, in each of the following eight sections, topics have been chosen for their interest to children and for their potential for stimulating scientific thinking and imagination rather than for their place in any developmental scheme in science. The eight categories of 'Science motivators' are, therefore, in no way offered as a substitute for the many excellent and comprehensive primary science schemes already available to schools.

'Hands-on' experience is a vital part of primary science and children should be encouraged whenever possible to handle scientifically interesting objects and make working models. Knowing how things work and developing the ability to mend mechanical devices is an extremely useful skill and should not be regarded as the exclusive or particular province of boys. Many of the more important aspects of mechanics can be introduced in the primary school before girls become unduly influenced by the conventional roles and subtle pressures society exerts upon them.

Many topics of scientific interest do not have convenient objects that children can handle individually so that it may be preferable on occasion for the teacher to perform an experiment or demonstration before the class.

However, excessive preoccupation with sense experience can sometimes be a substitute for, rather than a stimulus to, imaginative thinking and therefore not all the suggestions made in this chapter involve children in 'hands-on' experience. Our concern in this chapter is with purposeful scientific thinking—thinking with the aim of enriching scientific experience or extending scientific knowledge. This being so, we should not neglect the part played by interesting facts about the world that the teacher can bring to children. Facts are the building bricks with which the mind constructs theories and hypotheses. If ideas are to be generated then children's minds must have a store of basic facts of an exciting and stimulating nature with which to work, in addition to an understanding of how those facts might be related. These can provide children with a fund of knowledge that may stimulate hypothetical thinking and questioning.

Often, it is not feasible for the teacher to conduct interesting and significant scientific experiments, particularly with a large and heterogeneous class. If first-hand experience cannot be offered to the children, it may under some circumstances be better to present a topic through secondary sources rather than to omit that topic altogether. A number of such topics are suggested under the title of 'Popular scientific mysteries'.

Children should also be helped to see connections between science and other school subjects, connections within science itself and between the ideas and inventions of one scientist and those of another, albeit at a simple level.

Besides an involvement with the immediate objects and events of scientific interest, children should be given the opportunity to practise the processes of science—making hypotheses and considering the evidence for and against a particular idea. Planning simple experiments and investigations is a relatively sophisticated activity but the experimental method is an important aspect of science and some suggestions for developing this are given below.

MOTIVATORS FOR PRIMARY SCIENCE

There are a considerable number of books dealing with the scientific topics suggested in this chapter, many of them published in an extremely attractive format. A small sample only of these is noted in the 'Resources' section but browsing through any teachers' centre library or bookshop will reveal a great many more, although of varying quality.

Each section below contains a range of examples that can be adapted by teachers along some of the lines suggested in the hope that both children and teachers may enjoy a meaningful experience of 'science' in whatever situation they teach. The activities discussed are as follows.

- Asking questions
- Discussing popular science mysteries
- Performing unusual experiments
- Investigating the environment

- Constructing working models
- Studying interesting objects
- Making connections
- Learning amazing facts

ASKING QUESTIONS

What is it? Where does it come from? How does it work? The scientific spirit is above all a questioning one and questions are a child's expression of an inner urge to explore and find out. This instinct to know is strongest when children are young, and for this reason science in the primary school can be one of the most fascinating of subjects when curiosity is satisfied and the pleasure of finding out is experienced. For many less able children, however, curiosity and a questioning attitude need to be fostered and encouraged. For such children it may be useful to make questions 'person centred' rather than subject centred. For example, instead of asking 'What is a glacier made of?' the question can be asked 'What do you think it would be like walking on a glacier?'

Closed questions, which have just one correct answer, can also deter less able children from answering. For example 'Why does the water level fall in a pan of boiling water?' could be rephrased as an *open* question, namely 'What can you tell me about the water in the pan?' The answers to closed questions are either right or wrong. The answers to open questions do not require an absolute judgement to be made but ask for the child's opinion on the matter.

Certain situations are more question-provoking than others and these should be exploited whenever they arise in the natural course of events. The following are examples of question-provoking situations.

1. *Interesting objects* can stimulate meaningful and specific questions and a genuine desire to know. How does it move the wheel? What's inside the little box?
2. *Unusual conditions* often provoke questions. What is a rainbow? What makes the lightning? Why is it foggy?
3. *New experiences*—What's it like inside your body? (After a visit to the doctor's.) How do fish sleep? (After passing a stream.)
4. *Careful observation* of an event. Why does your hair sometimes crackle when you comb it? Why does a compass always point the same way? Where does the moon go in the daytime?
5. *When imagination is stimulated* children can ask more sophisti-

cated questions. What happens to our food when we eat it? What happens when animals die? What would happen if you kept heating something hotter and hotter . . . for ever? What is it really like in tropical Africa?

6. Some questions arise in the *natural course of events*. Why won't the car work? Why won't the tap come on?

7. Questions can be made the basis of *classroom games*. For example, an unknown object is shaken inside a box. What does it sound like? Will it roll? Is it very heavy? Variations of *Twenty Questions* can be played to encourage children to ask meaningful questions.

It is not always practicable to wait for children to ask questions and teachers should use their own judgement as to how best to stimulate them. However, if the right circumstances are created then children will nevertheless enjoy hearing what may be a prepared 'answer' to a question raised by the teacher. Answers to specific questions are, of course, only 'starters' and are not a substitute for a more detailed treatment of a topic. Some of the sorts of questions that may be usefully exploited are given below.

1. *What is a* . . . meteor, glacier, mirage, eclipse, planet, star, fossil, stalagmite/stalactite, vacuum, syphon . . .?

2. *Why do* . . . boats float, plants need water, stars move at night, people wear glasses, brakes get hot, voices echo, tides come twice a day, we oil things, make pan-handles of plastic . . .?

3. *Why does* . . . lightning strike, a wheelbarrow move a heavy load, a compass always point North . . .?

4. *What's it like* . . . under the sea, on the moon, under the soil, inside your body . . .?

5. *What happens when* . . . we jump off things, water freezes, objects are heated, we dig to the centre of the earth, we plant a seed upside down . . .?

6. *Do you know* . . . what makes sugar dissolve faster, how fast are your reactions, how to measure the height of a tree, how much air you breathe out, why we have day and night, what objects a magnet will attract . . .?

7. *Can you* . . . read by touch, make iron float, tell the time by the sun . . .?

DISCUSSING POPULAR SCIENCE MYSTERIES

Many great scientific discoveries began as 'mysteries'—inexplicable events that did not fit into the framework of science existing at that time. Children love mysteries, and publishers and film makers have been quick to recognise and exploit this interest. Many popular books now deal with the 'scientific evidence' for the existence of UFOs (unidentified flying objects), the Abominable Snowman, ESP (extra-sensory perception) and other well-known pseudo-scientific phe-nomena, and often suggest rational explanations for these. Science teaching should exploit and encourage children's natural interests in these topics for these make ideal vehicles for serious and reasoned class discussion. Since children like mysteries, they enjoy talking about them and a whole class can discuss the merits and likelihood of a particular theory or explanation.

The skills of the teacher will be much needed here, first to show a genuine interest and enthusiasm for the topic, and second to guide the discussion along rational scientific lines. Children soon recognise a genuine commitment by the teacher and, therefore, discussions should only be attempted by a well-prepared, informed and enthu-siastic teacher. End of term is often a suitable time for such debates. The blackboard can be used effectively to display the evidence for each of two contrasting theories.

Discussion may not lead to any definite conclusion but it will raise all sorts of interesting scientific ideas in children to which they will eventually find their own answers. It will provide a basis on which children can build when they come to consider science in a more formal and systematic fashion. Discussion might centre on the ques-tion of whether frogs and seeds could *really* fall from the sky. Does it depend on the strength of the wind (was it a whirlwind perhaps)? What about a huge block of ice that once fell? Where could that have originated? How big are the biggest hailstones that anyone in the class has seen? What about fireballs? The possibilities for discussion of bizarre happenings that seem to contradict scientific laws are endless.

The ultimate truth regarding such questions is not relevant here and neither are the personal beliefs of the teacher. What is important is that children should be persuaded to listen to and consider objec-tively both sides of a scientific argument: which one accords most closely with the known facts? In order to know what is contradictory, children must know what is feasible and 'scientific'. For example, is there a way to finally answer a question one way or another? The 'right' answer is the one that accords most closely with the facts at the child's disposal, as indeed is the 'rightness' of any scientific theory— see, for example, Jos Elstgeest's article (1985). Children must adopt a critical but open mind to the evidence presented and be challenged for reasons why they believe what they do. Are the reasons really valid? Have we considered *all* the factors involved? Teachers must be prepared to admit that they don't know all the answers—but then neither do the scientists.

Teaching organisation

How the topics are introduced will depend on teaching style. A whole-class approach works well provided children are mature enough to listen to each other's points of view. The level to which teachers want to take the subject will, of course, depend on the interest and abilities of the class. These subjects provide excellent topics for children to write about, and to express their own ideas. A topic could be introduced through an interesting true story dealing with the strange or incredible. Children of all ability levels are fascinated by good stories, and to hold the attention of distractable or hyperactive children is a worthwhile aim whatever the subject-matter.

Below are some suggestions for topics suitable for class discussion. Many of these topics have been written about widely at a popular level and many colourful and informative books are now available (see Resources).

Can animals talk?
What do animals say to each other? Can we communicate with them? Can we teach apes to ask questions? Do animals *think* as we do? What do we mean by communication?
(*Topics*   Communication, environmental studies.)

How do animals find their way about?
How do salmon, birds, butterflies and other animals migrate? How have some pets found their way home after covering hundreds or even thousands of miles?
(*Topics*   The earth's magnetism, animal scents, navigating by the stars, animal instincts.)

What makes a human being human?
Cases of children brought up by wild animals (e.g. the Bengal 'wolf girls'. The 'wild boy' of Aveyron).
(*Topics*   The relation of man to his natural environment; food, warmth, clothing, security, etc.)

Who controls the ant cities?
Do ants *think* about what they are doing? Do soldier ants really protect the nest? Will one ant 'sacrifice' itself for another one? What is

instinct? Is it always 'blind'? Other animals and insects with social organisations.

Can people really see things that aren't there?
Famous illusions and hallucinations. Children make their own optical illusions. Can we make cold water seem warm?
(*Topics*   The five senses, the human body.)

Did a giant meteorite fall in central Siberia?
What caused the explosion? Could it have been a lump of ice? An asteroid? A fireball? A comet? What is the evidence?
(*Topics*   Weather, astronomy.)

Are there really such things as UFOs?
What are the possible alternatives? Planets, meteorites, cloud formations, reflections, planes, helicopters or even swarms of flying ants.

Do unknown creatures still roam the earth and oceans?
The vastness of the oceans and chance of detection. Could a lost world exist? Could dinosaurs still exist? Have any 'extinct' creatures ever been found? What is a hairy mammoth, a great auk, a dodo?
(*Topic*   Environmental studies.)

Can the moon influence plants, animals and man?
How does the moon influence the tides? What effect does it have on the growth of plants, the cycles of insects and the behaviour of certain crabs and turtles? How can the moon affect human statistics? Does gravitational pull affect the chemistry of our bodies? Could the planets affect us in some way? What is astrology?

What will life be like in the future?
Will there be thinking robots? Will computers ever be able to think? Could we plant microcomputers in animals? Could we build a bionic man? Could we produce a half-ape/half-man that could be trained to help us?
(*Topic*   Communication.)

PERFORMING UNUSUAL EXPERIMENTS

By 'unusual' experiments we mean those experiments in which either the performance of the experiment is particularly interesting to observe or the outcome is entirely unexpected. Unusual experiments, like unusual objects, are remembered by children. For example, who can forget seeing a tin-can crushed by an invisible force we called air pressure?

Interesting experiments can often be introduced by provocative questions. For example, consider the following questions.

- Can you pick up a piece of paper without touching it?
- Can you float a steel needle on water?
- Can you put an egg into a narrow-necked bottle without breaking it?
- Can you break a ruler(!) with a sheet of newspaper?
- Can you put a candle out without touching or blowing it?
- Can you crush a tin without touching it?

If the experiment seems to be more in the form of a scientific 'trick', then so much the better. Children will remember and talk about the unusual trick, particularly if it is one that can be performed in front of relatives or friends in the home environment.

Teachers will doubtless have their own favourite 'happenings' but here are some of the writer's. These are merely reminders of a few simple experiments, details of which can be found from many sources (see Resources).

Static electricity

Put some crumbs or Rice Krispies in a saucer and cover with cling film. Rub the cling film with a dry paper-towel to make them dance. Now try bringing another rubbed piece of cling film near to the first.

Suspend a butterfly of tin foil on a pin inside a thin plastic carton. Rub the carton to move the tin foil. Now bring your hands *near* to the carton and cause it to move again (psychokinesis!).

Shuffle with slippers on a nylon carpet. Get someone to lean against a metal radiator, then touch the end of their nose.

Comb your hair with a plastic comb and hold it near to running water.

Electricity

Pass a current along a short, thin piece of wire, suspended pendulum-like between the two poles of a magnet. The wire should rest loosely on a metal contact at the base of the pendulum and this will vibrate as the current is passed through. The explanation is not important at this stage—the movement *is*!

Make a simple nail electromagnet.

Magnetism

Attach a paper-clip to a piece of cotton and suspend the clip in the air by using a magnet.

Tap iron filings into a pattern above a bar magnet.

Make a floating-bar magnet compass on a cork.

Sound

Make small objects bounce on a drum or pieces of paper on a violin string.

Bounce a ping-pong ball off a tuning fork.

Make a tin-can and string telephone.

Air

Make a diver in a bottle of water rise and float by altering the pressure of air above the surface.

Put a candle in a jar and extinguish it with carbon dioxide made from vinegar and bicarbonate of soda.

Fill a tin with steam and let air pressure crush it.

Light

Make a rainbow with a prism.

Place mirrors opposite to each other and produce an infinity of images.

Water

Soak a piece of cloth in a strong solution of salt, suspend it from the four corners and place an egg in the centre. Now burn the handkerchief and the egg will remain suspended in the centre of the salt handkerchief.

Lift an ice cube by resting a piece of string on the surface of the ice and adding salt.

Float a needle or steel washer on the 'skin' of water.

Chemistry

Blow the cork out of a bottle using vinegar and bicarbonate of soda.

Dissolve salt in water until a naphthalene moth-ball just floats. Add tap water until it sinks. Stir in a teaspoon of bicarbonate of soda. Add more moth-balls and then a spoonful of vinegar. The moth-balls will rise and fall with the attached carbon dioxide.

Write invisibly with lemon juice. Warm the paper to reveal the writing.

INVESTIGATING THE ENVIRONMENT

Primary school science investigations need to be no more than systematic attempts to find out something. Most young children are not interested in *methods* of enquiry, only in the materials utilised and the results of that investigation. The end result of an investigation should, therefore, answer a question asked by children. General methods of enquiry will begin to emerge in a natural way when more than one investigation has been conducted and techniques will become more efficient as the children gain experience. An investigation should be a sustained enquiry and such a study can only be successfully carried out in classroom conditions if the children are sufficiently motivated.

A particularly fruitful source of interesting questions for investigation is the natural environment: insects or 'minibeasts' and all forms of growing things. Insects are always available, easy to acquire and cost nothing to keep. There are reckoned to be a million known species of insects and as many unknown, so studies can be made that are unlikely to have been carried out before. Note can be made of an insect's direction of crawl. Will it resume that direction when temporarily disorientated? What caused it to change direction? How can its speed of movement be altered? These and many other questions can be investigated.

Many living creatures have the capacity to respond not only to changes in light and temperature but also to the very weak magnetic and electrostatic fields of the earth. Some may even be influenced by minute changes in the gravitational pull of the moon and planets and children can keep a note, for example, of the phases of the moon in conjunction with the responses of plants.

Colonies of ants kept in a formicarium will provide a fascinating source of study, and many books give instructions for their proper upkeep. Fungi and moulds are another rich potential source of untried experimental investigations and over 100,000 species are *known* to exist! Plants establish fixed patterns of responses to the daily rhythm of light and warmth, and these make ideal subjects of study for individual children who may be relatively immobile. For example, children confined to wheelchairs could assume sole responsibility for observing and noting these slow and relatively small responses.

In all investigations of the behaviour of living creatures children should experience a sense of wonder at the essential mystery of life and teachers should instil a respect for all living things since the extent of the feelings of insects and lower animals is still unknown. No expensive resources are required for any of these investigations (see Resources; Womack, 1986) but a variety of books should be made available to guide the children's and the teacher's directions of investigations.

CONSTRUCTING WORKING MODELS

'Nature' is no longer the familiar environment it used to be for most children. Today, a child's world is one of mechanical devices: washing-machines, cars, video-recorders, bikes, computer games and remote-controlled dolls. Television has given much publicity to innovative model-making with such series as 'The Great Egg Race', and these reflect a growing interest in and appreciation of the skill and inventiveness of the participants. Models emphasise working mechanical principles rather than concepts and therefore demonstrate the technological aspect of science. Models made by children at school and subsequently taken home are a source of pride and a focus of attention from parents and friends.

Getting children to think about how they would make a model house or car will inevitably create much discussion. Play with models often leads to comparison of performance and measurement (for example, which is the best shape of sail or size of wheel? Which is the most stable design or most streamlined shape?).

Small individual models may be made by the whole class at the same time if sufficient materials are available. Templates to draw round and cut out are often necessary to alleviate organisational problems in such a style of working. Alternatively, children may work in small groups but this is less satisfactory since only one child will be able to take the model home.

Another style of teaching is to have available a large quantity of 'scrap' materials that the children can take and use in their own way. Alternatively, children can be asked to bring in their own unwanted materials. Miscellaneous sizes of wood offcuts, hammers, nails and pliers are useful tools and materials for this style of working.

Models such as string telephones, windmills, balloon-propelled planes, elastic-powered boats, spinning cardboard discs on string (with the colours of the rainbow), 3-D glasses, spinning card with bird on one side and cage on the other (the bird appears to be in the cage), etc., can conveniently be made in any classroom using only material from school stock. Full construction details of these and other models can be found in a number of excellent books (see Resources).

Toys

A useful source of scientific ideas and principles is broken toys that children can be invited to bring in to mend. Practice can be given in taking the toys to pieces and checking the working of individual parts. Visual examination of components for faults is a valuable exercise and it is not always necessary for the teacher to diagnose the fault. Children should be encouraged to take responsibility for solving the problem themselves, however imperfect their repair may be.

Moving toys illustrate well the principle of cause and effect. For example, things move because they are pushed or pulled. Some materials only pull (string), whilst others only push (liquids). Springs can both pull and push. Some causes of movement are visible (a lever, a cog wheel), whilst others are invisible (such as air pressure or magnetism).

Children will discover for themselves that some effects have more than one cause and similarly some causes have more than one effect. These ideas need not be taught explicitly but children should be made aware of them through extensive experience with mechanical gadgets.

STUDYING INTERESTING OBJECTS

The important role objects play in children's learning is widely recognised. An object is concrete and tangible—a magnet, a camera, a telescope, a periscope. An object explains itself. Questions can be asked about it: What does it do? How does it move? What is inside? If the object is a machine of some kind: How does it work? or even, Why does it work? If it is a broken toy then it may be necessary to find out how it works in order to mend it.

Some years ago, the writer conducted a small-scale research project into what young slow-learning children remembered best after viewing a primary mathematics television programme. During the course of one programme, the presenter carried out two distinct operations concerning measurement. First, she measured her forearm and a short time later she measured a pair of yellow wellingtons with a stick. Subsequent questioning of the large class of children viewing the programme showed that whereas almost all the children clearly remembered the measuring of the wellingtons, only three recalled the presenter's action in measuring her arm. It would appear that the children remembered the action of measuring the wellingtons because of the 'unexpected' objects involved. It seems likely that children relate to objects much more readily than they do to actions, particularly if the objects are unusual or interesting. This is not a phenomenon peculiar to children (as every journalist knows) and teachers can exploit this by an imaginative selection of objects and materials for discussion. (If concepts are introduced through the medium of interesting objects that children can see, touch or hear, then the concept is more likely to be recalled in association with that object. Although it may not always be possible to find a suitable object related directly to the concept the teacher has in mind, it may be found advantageous on occasion to use an object that is only *indirectly* associated with the idea but that nevertheless has a high interest value.

The few suggestions below are of relatively familiar objects, which have been used by this writer in the classroom. The most interesting objects are usually unique to the teacher (for example, a Victorian mechanical working model of a piano player). The exact mode of operation of some of the items listed may involve principles beyond the grasp of some pupils but children will bring to an exploration of any object their own knowledge, needs and level of understanding.

For convenience, some of the objects have been listed under conventional primary science topic headings.

Light, lenses, mirrors

Old camera, binoculars, telescope, microscope, magnifying glass, 3-D glasses, periscope.

Mechanical forces

Old spring-powered clock or watch, model steam-engine, mechanical door-bell, bicycle bell, car jack, lock and key, old mileometer, speedometer, a wind-up toy.

Air

Model parachute, balloon or balloon-powered toy, bicycle or car foot-pump, toy glider, aerosol spray (with rubber bulb).

Water

Toy submarine, battery-powered model boats, chemical 'flowers' that open in water.

Magnetism, electricity

Torch, compass, old radio, battery-powered tape-recorder, electric-motor driven toys.

Old objects

Stamps, coins, fossils, medals, 'Victoriana'.

Natural objects

Insects (dead or alive), shells, sea-horse, starfish, horse-chestnuts, seeds.

MAKING CONNECTIONS

It is widely accepted that one of the most important factors in children's learning is what they already know. If, therefore, new concepts are introduced through familiar contexts or linked to ideas that are already understood, then learning will be considerably enhanced. Science is an ideal subject to make connections with many other parts of the curriculum—geography, for example, through study of the geographical distribution of different plants and animals, the migration routes of birds or the study of weather conditions. Historically, children can study the way the wheel and other mechanical devices have been used to build roads and castles or to wage war. Art and craft are involved in the making of models or using of mechanical devices such as the harmonograph to produce mathematical patterns.

Mathematics can be related to science in many ways including the following.

1. Measurement of size, speed, weight, etc. of both plants and animals. For example, measuring the speed of travel of a snail.
2. A study of the mathematical shapes found in nature (spirals in shells and climbing plants, tesselating shapes—hexagons in honeycombs, spirals in sunflower heads, etc.
3. Symmetry found in animals, leaves, insects, etc.
4. Counting, sampling and estimating in science.
5. Measuring mechanical forces – speed, amplitude, etc.

Within science itself, links can be made. For example, in one of the author's classes a topic was begun on weather in view of a particularly heavy spell of rain. Interest focused on rain and water until the children saw, on a schools' television mathematics programme, a funicular railway in the south of England, powered by water from a stream. Discussion then centred on water-powered machines, which led eventually to the teacher bringing his own model steam-engine into the classroom. This was operated by most of the children in the class. Mechanical attachments could be fitted to the engine and this resulted in various other kinds of mechanical toys being brought along by the children. The topic came round to a consideration of the speeds of different vehicles and the speed records set up in different sports. This involved a good deal of mathematics in the area of measurement. Streamlining was investigated and model streamlined sports-cars were brought in. (One of the children's mothers drove a streamlined sports car!) The cars contained battery-powered electric motors and time was spent on fixing up various electric motors detached from their toys. Batteries were investigated and a natural halt came to the connected series of 'science' diversions with a look inside battery-powered calculators.

These 'lessons' did not set out to investigate systematically any particular science topic but were more in the nature of 'hands-on' discussion groups that followed the children's interests as they arose.

Many interesting connections can be made between the ideas of one scientist or inventor and another and this has been used as a basis for a television series of the same name ('Connections'). However, connections in children's minds are not usually the same ones that the teacher might make. Children's ideas are linked more by fortuitous association or interest and teachers should occasionally allow time to follow these up.

LEARNING AMAZING FACTS

Children have a great interest in extremes. What would happen if it carried on forever? How long is the longest . . .? What was the biggest ever . . .? World records in many areas of human endeavour are listed in the well-known *Guinness Book of Records* (see Resources). Suggestions and ideas for some of the more interesting and fantastic aspects of the natural and human world are given below.

Facts about mankind

Personal attributes—tallest, fattest, heaviest, oldest, longest hair, nails, beard . . . smallest, lightest, thinnest . . .
Statistics—most children, wives; population figures; numbers killed by snakes . . .
Sports records—times, distances, speeds, size . . .
Daring feats—height and length of tight-rope walk over the Niagara Falls, highest dive, greatest height jumping from plane (without a parachute!) . . .

Facts about animals

Migrating animals—distances, directions, times, speeds . . .
Hibernating animals—time sleeping, rate of breathing, body temperature . . .
Ants—number in a colony, size of the termitary, eggs laid per day . . .
Animal records—largest insect, longest snake, smallest bird . . .

Facts about the earth

The greatest explosion (Krakatoa)—height and distance to which rocks were thrown, distance away that noise was heard, number of people killed, number of ships destroyed . . .
Tidal waves—height, speed, width, geographical occurrence, ships destroyed . . .
Earthquakes—number of earthquakes, Richter scale, physical effects, powerful forces . . .
Journey to the centre of the earth—the earth's crust, distance to the centre, rate of increase of temperature, effect of gravity (at the centre of the earth!) . . .
Meteorites—the great Siberian meteorite: height and diameter of fire from accounts, number of trees flattened . . .
Volcanoes—rate of growth of a new volcano, temperature of lava, angle of slope, length of lava tubes formed . . .
Records—deepest mine, highest mountain, deepest sea, tallest building . . .

   Great scientific discoveries and the lives of certain famous scientists can also be of interest to children if a popular 'story book' approach is used (see Resources).

PART III
Evaluation and Teaching

6

Evaluation and teaching in science

AIMS, PLANNING AND EVALUATION

The need for planning in science is great since children's needs, a teacher's professional requirements and social pressures from industry and parents vary from year to year and class to class. Planning need not cramp the style of teachers who wish to adapt their teaching to the current needs and interests of the class, but in the absence of such inspiration there should be some record of what the teacher intends to do or what has already been carried out. It is the experience of the writer and probably most experienced teachers that a well-planned scheme of work will pay dividends in terms of both children's learning and teacher stress!

The content of primary science

Should we teach children facts about the physical world or should we rather show them how to discover relationships between things? Learning facts is frequently contrasted with understanding the processes of science but the distinction is not nearly so clear in the classroom context. The distinction is exaggerated further when 'process science' is equated with learning by discovery while facts are assumed to be taught by rote methods. This makes an unnecessary and somewhat artificial division between two approaches to teaching, a division that rarely exists in such a stark form. Indeed Paul Black (1980) has argued persuasively that the science as process approach may have been somewhat over-emphasised and can sometimes be *too* processed to allow children to classify and interpret facts in their own way.

HMI (DES, 1984) go some way in support of this view when they state that 'There are certain fundamental facts and ideas that pupils must meet and grasp if they are to make any significant progress in their studies'. Learning facts about the world is a relatively easy task for children of average or below average ability and this can instil in them a sense of pride and self-confidence, qualities which are often lacking in slower learning children. Learning about interesting scientific happenings and properties of objects which it is not possible to bring into a school classroom does have a place in primary science and complements those concepts acquired experientially. Moreover, once learnt, particular scientific facts can become the specific examples from which the learner can abstract and generalise. In this way it is possible for children to discover for themselves a link between items of information. It is not always necessary to handle physically materials in order to make 'discoveries'. Science can be learned in more than one way.

Aims and teaching

A distinction sometimes made is that between deductive and inductive learning. In the former, the teacher explains to the children a principle or concept and then supplies several examples of that concept exemplified in different situations, while in the latter, teachers are encouraged to provide many different examples of a concept and then lead children to 'discover' the common principle for themselves.

However, for less able children, neither of these approaches to learning the concepts of science is easy. For example, although many slower learning children may eventually come to understand how steam from water in a kettle condenses onto a cold plate to form water again, they may fail to see this same process at work in the formation of clouds or in situations they have not previously encountered.

We do not know whether children think predominantly deductively (from a generalisation to particular examples) or inductively (from particular examples to a general principle). These are primarily philosophical distinctions that fail to take into account the full complexity of any practical learning or teaching situation. In fact, children can and do make sense of the world in their own way and build up their own mental framework for understanding the world, with or without the help of science teaching.

An example of such an 'alternative framework', given by Michael Watts (1982), is that of the child who believed that gravity *increased* with distance from the surface of the earth, reaching its maximum and therefore forming a barrier at the upper limit of the earth's atmosphere. This explained why a ball thrown upwards comes back again as though it was being forced upwards into an invisible sponge. It also explained why space rockets need an 'escape velocity' in order to break through this barrier.

This was a perfectly reasonable explanation of the facts at the child's disposal, though the theory was unlikely to have arisen as a result of either an inductive or deductive consideration of the facts. Children's existing frameworks may be a help or a hindrance to our science teaching but we would do well to note them and learn from them.

An important aim of science teaching is to develop in children a receptivity to all possible experiences and an openness to new ideas. In seeming contrast to this, scientific investigation sometimes begins with a specific question requiring single-mindedness and perseverance for its solution. With such a problem, children may need to be shown how to consider only those factors relevant to the question and to suspend belief in those ideas that have not yet been proven. Science teaching has the difficult task of steering a course between these two contrasting attitudes to scientific investigation.

Therefore, no single method of teaching science can be advocated as more suitable than others for teaching children with learning difficulties. Our aim should be to teach children to be flexible and to analyse each problem in its own way. However, this is a long-term aim and one that is not easy to put into practice in the primary school classroom. In the classroom, teachers should have more practical aims; children should be handling materials, discovering their properties and observing their behaviour under different conditions. There should be much discussing and recording of information— teachers should be encouraging children to generalise about happenings not yet observed and to offer explanations as to why things behave as they do. At a later stage, children should attempt to carry out simple experiments to 'see what happens' or to test an idea. At a still more advanced stage the children may make hypotheses to explain a set of results or to predict what may happen under certain conditions.

In summary, children learning science in the primary school should be:

- Observing and classifying.
- Measuring and recording.
- Generalising and reasoning.
- Hypothesising and experimenting.

Evaluation and pupils' progress

Before evaluation of pupils is carried out there must be agreement among teachers as to both the purpose and the interpretation of that evaluative procedure. Evaluation is only a means to an end and if the aim of the evaluation is to improve teaching, then provision should be made for possible revision of the syllabus to take place with a minimum of administrative formalities. If the outcome of the evaluation is unlikely to be acted upon then the procedure is best abandoned and the time saved devoted to improving teaching based on a more intuitive assessment of learning needs.

Evaluation can be related to the effectiveness of the teaching and also to the progress pupils make. For example, evaluation may have the aim of discovering whether children have gained in understanding as a result of teaching and therefore whether certain children need special help. A further reason for evaluation may be in order to provide continuity of teaching for children who, through no fault of their own, may have changed schools or teachers a disproportionate number of times.

Attention should also be given to discovering the strengths as well as the weaknesses of children and these strengths can then be built on or used to boost a child's confidence. For example, asking a slower learning child to explain something he *does* understand to a child who *doesn't* may work wonders for his self-esteem and confidence.

Assuming that we wish to carry out some form of evaluation, how might this best be achieved? This is a difficult task in science. Informal evaluation can be through checklists, interviews, saving children's work, situational evaluation, children's interests, recall of information, multi-choice questions, etc. In addition many of the excellent primary science schemes (for example, *Science 5–13*, see Resources) have their own systems for recording work completed by children although these may not always indicate difficulties in understanding. This is particularly so when children have been working in groups, for group work often 'carries' less able children.

Diagnosis of difficulties children may be experiencing is most effectively carried out by some form of continuous monitoring. Immediate help can then be given in the situation where the problem first becomes apparent. HMI (DES, 1984) recognise the need for evaluation of some sort but admit that in most schools science is not assessed. They suggest that the teacher should know in detail the range of work already encountered by each pupil, the level at which it has been tackled and how successful pupils have been in mastering the ideas and knowledge involved.

Pupil records

Good records make a significant contribution to evaluation but information recorded should be both necessary and sufficient for the purpose intended. Recording detailed evaluations of individual children's scientific attitudes and accomplishments can take much of a teacher's time and unless this information is intended to be acted upon, such evaluation is sometimes counterproductive in a busy classroom.

Some proposed evaluation schemes contain up to a dozen different attitudes and skills to be recorded for each child in the class but such a detailed record sheet encourages only the most general of comments that are often meaningless and at worst can become out of date and therefore inaccurate. It is not usually necessary to make detailed comments on those children who do not give undue cause for concern, for this formality inevitably takes a teacher's time away from those children who really need it.

Some assessment instruments have columns to indicate attitudes and skills such as *curiosity, interests, observation, co-operation, drawing conclusions, listening, asking questions, making predictions,* etc., but unless each of these is related to a specific scientific topic, these will yield little real information about the child. A child's attitude to a topic depends to a great extent on his interest in that topic. For example, some children show a great interest and learning capacity for the scientific study of pets but little interest in, say, magnetism. The point has been made that competence at skills cannot be transferred from one topic to another but depends on both content and context (Jenkins, 1987).

Children's attitudes to science are important but for practical purposes it may be sufficient to record the degree to which this is either positive or negative. Significant changes in attitude can be noted on the reverse of a formal record sheet in addition to any professional evaluation, help or counselling that may have been given.

Two other important aspects to consider in recording are the *content* of science that has been assimilated and the use by children of various scientific skills such as observation, classification or reasoning. For example, a record sheet might indicate the extent of acquisition of a concept or skill by the degree of shading on a rectangle. For example, [▨▢] would indicate an average assessment that may be given in the absence of any information to the contrary.

For each science topic taught, one column can indicate how well the content has been learnt, another column how effectively scientific

Figure 6.1 *Example of possible science record sheet*

Topic (for example, weather)	SCIENCE RECORD SHEET		
Name	Knowledge and learning	Use of scientific skills	Attitude and interest shown

skills have been used and another can record whether the child's attitude has been positive or negative to the teaching of that particular topic. One class sheet can be used to cover each topic and then at a glance can be seen those topics the class have enjoyed (see Figure 6.1). A more comprehensive discussion of checklists for recording children's progress in science is given in the Schools Council Project, *Progress in Learning Science* (Harlen, Darwin and Murphy, 1977). It is not so important to find the 'right' system as it is for the staff and headteacher to agree upon a common policy with regard to recording and for this to be used and acted upon in a consistent and meaningful way.

Children's recording of work

Children should be encouraged to record in some form the results of their work in drawing, writing, models, displays, friezes, etc., for this stimulates both discussion and mental reflection. This is also an opportunity to display more prominently the work of less able children who may need this encouragement.

Although there are sound educational reasons for children writing their own account of an experiment or activity, for many children this is a major undertaking. The effort required to concentrate on the form of writing as well as the content may be too much and help may have to be given. Partially completed workcards are useful for this or the blackboard can be used to note down a series of instructions for children to follow. The use of a simple word-processing computer could also be considered for children whose writing is very poor.

Teachers should be clear in such cases what the objectives of a written task are. In many cases a carefully chosen picture may be worth a thousand words and much can be learned by both teacher and pupil from the explanatory diagrams that illustrate many of the popular children's magazines. Using coloured chalk on a blackboard is a very effective way of holding a class's attention and children are usually extremely complimentary about any pictures teachers might attempt to draw. At the very worst, less able children may be heartened to see the obvious imperfections in a teacher's artistic improvisations!

CLASSROOM PRACTICE

Teaching styles

It is not necessary or even desirable to adopt a single teaching style for science and whether a whole class or a group approach is taken will depend on the subject-matter and availability of apparatus.

The advantages of whole class teaching are that children's ideas can be shared among the whole class and background information can also be disseminated more effectively than if the children are put in groups. Also when performing one experiment before the whole class, there is more certainty of the principle involved being effectively demonstrated. A major disadvantage is, however, the difficulty of gauging the extent of involvement of all the children.

Working in groups, children become more involved and must take more responsibility for the results of their work. They are often able to choose to some extent the work they carry out. Opportunities arise for the more able to explain to the less able children and there is more co-operation and individuality expressed. Listening to one group of children explaining to the class an experiment they have performed can give a teacher valuable ideas for future work in science, apart from the beneficial effects on the children concerned. Listening to one child explaining to another can be equally illuminating. A disadvantage of this way of working is that some children may be 'carried' by the rest of the group and it requires skill and perception on the part of the teacher to detect when this is happening.

A convenient method of group working is to have (say) five groups of three children carrying out one activity whilst another set of five groups of three carry out a second activity. At the mid-point of the lesson, each set of groups exchange activities. This could be carried out within one lesson period or two. If more varied apparatus and activities are available, then the number of groups carrying out the same activity at the same time can be lessened, although this will necessitate more careful organisation. An advantage of restricting the number of activities taking place at the same time is that more meaningful discussions can take place later with the whole class.

Continuity of theme should not be pursued at the expense of losing interest. Variety sustains motivation and a flexible teacher should always be ready to adapt to the interests of the class. The classroom organisation that allows children to explore freely the material to hand and to talk about their results as work proceeds will provide an ideal learning environment for most children.

Workcards can be useful for a class of wide ability range if used with discretion, but care should be taken that those workcards dealing with important or difficult concepts are not systematically ignored by the children. For this purpose a record should be kept of cards completed and teachers should check that if a card is temporarily in use by other children, then this will not affect the comprehension of subsequent cards. Another danger of workcards is the tendency for this type of work to develop into a race and teachers should ensure that rapid completion of cards does not result in any benefits for a 'fast' group.

Generally, there should be sufficient materials for all the children in the class, since children deprived of the object in which they are interested become frustrated. Materials should be available at the start of the lesson and if the lesson is a relatively unstructured one then plenty of follow-up ideas should be available—in case there is a shortage of ideas from the children themselves. A well-kept and frequently updated science corner with charts, displays and collections of miscellaneous 'science' objects is usually appreciated by children. A 'browsers welcome' sign could be prominently displayed on the table.

Lesson planning

Science is probably the most difficult of all subjects in which to adopt a regular lesson format, the format depending so much on the subject-matter of the lesson. However, there are certain aspects that should be considered when planning any science lesson although all of these aspects need not necessarily be involved in the preparation of any one lesson. By way of example, these considerations are illustrated below by reference to two specific topics—*air* and *magnetism*. Such a list of suggestions is not, of course, exhaustive since each teacher brings to the lesson his or her own particular expertise, knowledge and style. The following is therefore in no way intended to suggest a pattern for science teaching, only perhaps to suggest how a wider range of ideas in any one topic may be stimulated.

1. *Possible topic starters*
   Asking questions:
   Air Is there air on other planets?
   Magnetism Do magnets attract all metals?
   Discussing popular science mysteries:
   Air Can we identify all objects we see in the air (UFOs)?
   Magnetism Are ships' compasses affected within the Bermuda Triangle?
   Performing unusual experiments:
   Air Can you crush a tin can with air?
   Magnetism Attracting upwards a paper-clip attached to a piece of cotton.
   Investigating the environment:
   Air The breathing of hibernating animals.
   Magnetism Are insects affected by weak magnetism?
   Constructing working models:
   Air A cardboard windmill.
   Magnetism A cork floating-compass.

Studying an interesting object:
Air Car-tyre pump.
Magnetism Magnetic toy.
Making connections:
Air Making paint patterns by blowing through straws.
Magnetism Making patterns with iron filings.
Learning amazing facts:
Air The longest time for which a person can hold their breath.
Magnetism Places on the earth where magnets *don't* point North.

2. *Which difficult concepts are involved*
Air Air is a mixture of invisible gases.
Magnetism What exactly is magnetism?

3. *Possible teacher demonstrations*
Air Water held in an upturned glass by a card.
Magnetism Demonstration of an electromagnet.

4. *Interesting questions to ask*
Air Do all animals need air? Is air the same all over the earth? etc.
Magnetism How can you make one magnet from another?

5. *Activities for children*
Air Blowing up a balloon and releasing it.
Magnetism Groups attempt to make the longest chain of pin magnets, etc.

6. *Familiar applications*
Air Blowing up tyres, parachuting, wind-surfing, etc.
Magnetism A mariner's compass.

7. *Ideas for children's recording*
Air Children make a 'topic' book on air.
Magnetism Children draw in a book all objects they know containing magnets.

8. *Links with other subjects*
Air Geography—erosion by wind.
Maths—Beaufort Wind Speed Scale.
Magnetism Geography—the position of the magnetic North Pole.
Art—patterns of iron filings around the poles of a magnet.

9. *Further developments*
Air The weather, birds, wind-using sports, etc.
Magnetism Electro-magnets, electrostatic phenomena, battery electricity.

10. *Resources*
Books, charts, slides, films, etc., which are available.

SUPPLEMENTARY SCIENCE ACTIVITIES

A major problem when teaching classes of children of differing abilities is that of the children's different rates of working. Although work may be adapted to different levels, as suggested in Part II, it remains a very real problem to keep a proportion of a large class of children occupied usefully while others are completing the assigned activity, particularly if group work involves carrying out experiments.

It is useful to have in reserve a small selection of activities whose completion is not essential to the purpose of the lesson but which, nevertheless, can be related to the lesson theme. The following ideas can, for example, be used after a science lesson during the 'clearing-up' period. For each suggested activity, a simple example has been given. Teachers can make up their own examples to fit the topics they are teaching and the age and ability of individual classes.

Examples of supplementary activities

1. Letter squares
Find the science words hidden in the letter square. Words can begin anywhere and progress in a vertical, horizontal or diagonal straight line in any direction.

E	P	Q	A	M	B	H
N	R	E	T	A	W	E
E	D	M	F	G	V	A
R	I	A	M	N	E	T
G	H	L	C	E	G	L
Y	I	F	A	T	O	M
S	M	E	T	R	E	N

(Hidden words are:
MAGNET, HEAT, ENERGY,
WATER, AIR, FLAME
ATOM, METRE)

There are many variations of this puzzle format that are simple to construct. Some children can be asked to make up their own, using squared paper and incorporating words listed by the teacher. Pairs of children can make up puzzles and exchange them when complete.

2. Anagrams
Rearrange the letters in each box to make a scientific word.

NICE SEC (SCIENCE)   NEST IS CARE (RESISTANCE)

GET MAN (MAGNET)

3. *Find the questions*
Here are some *answers* to questions. What were the questions?

(a) Ice.   (d) Molecule.   (g) 32 °F.
(b) Hot.   (e) Element.   (h) Capillary.
(c) Friction.   (f) 100 °C.   (i) Convection.

4. *Word finding*
How many different words can you make from these words?

BATTERY   THERMOMETER   SCIENTIFIC

Although not strictly a scientific activity this is a very useful one for the 'clearing-up' period at the end of a science lesson.

5. *Codes*
This is the code.

1   2   3   4   5   6   7 8...
a   b   c   d   e   f   g h...

The following scientific words have been written in code. Can you find them?

(a) 9,3,5 (*Clue* Water at 0°C). *Answer* Ice.
(b) 6,12,1,13,5 (*Clue* A burning gas). *Answer* Flame.

6. *Chopping blocks*
Can you rearrange these six columns in order to make another block of the same size containing a scientific message?

Example 1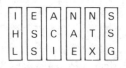

Solution 1   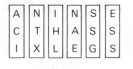   (An insect has six legs.)

Example 2   E   O   E   I   L   K   P   L
            T   A   T   A   S   T   R   C
            O   E   I   N   U   L   K   P
            L   P   R   E   L   S   E   E

Solution 2

L	I	K	E	P	O	L	E
S	A	T	T	R	A	C	T
U	N	L	I	K	E	P	O
L	E	S	R	E	P	E	L

(Like poles attract, unlike poles repel.)

These puzzles are easy to construct from a simple scientific statement, using squared paper. The number of letters in the sentence must not, however, be a prime number. Again, children can be asked to construct their own from a given sentence.

7. Jumbled sentences
Jumbled sentences containing jumbled words if necessary. For example, *make sirmp we a can warinob a using.*
(*Answer* We can make a rainbow using a prism.)

8. Crosswords

9. Quizwords
Answers to questions must be arranged horizontally to spell a word vertically (ice).

```
      t i n
      c h e m i c a l
m a g n e t
```

7

Evaluation and teaching in mathematics

PLANNING AND EVALUATION

Schemes of work

Preparing a scheme of work for the wide range of mathematical ability found in the average primary school class is not an easy task. HMI suggest that the content of mathematics should be 'differentiated' so that all pupils are challenged whatever their age or ability (DES, 1985). One way this may be achieved is to present the same content in different contexts to suit the differing levels of maturity and needs of children. For example, HMI suggest investigatory activities that can be adapted to different levels of ability, and several ideas for investigations are given in Chapters 3 and 4 of this book.

However, such practical and interesting approaches are often limited by the amount of work to be covered in the maths curriculum. This sometimes makes the expository style of teaching the only practical means of covering the syllabus. Allowance should therefore be made when planning a scheme of work for more flexible and imaginative teaching approaches when topics are to be tried out such as sport, space travel, 'large numbers', estimating or investigations, etc. Information should also be obtained on the availability of mathematical resources if the scheme is to be flexible enough to accommodate to the needs of all children. As the Cockcroft Report has suggested in the context of secondary education, the content of a scheme of work could be developed from a consideration of the needs of lower attaining pupils and then extended to encompass the needs of all children.

Guidelines for the teaching of mathematics are available from most LEAs and it is not the intention to outline a complete scheme of work here. Comprehensive evaluations of mathematics schemes, numeracy resources and structural apparatus currently available are provided by several authorities, for example, *Ways and Means* (Somerset

Education Authority, 1981). This includes a review of the highly structured *Distar Arithmetic* programme (see Bibliography).

The following sections outline possible schemes of work together with suggestions for evaluation under the separate headings of Number, Measure, Spatial Concepts and Logic. Summary lists indicate the main topics within each of these mathematical areas that should be considered when planning a scheme.

Evaluation

Well-thought-out evaluative procedures in mathematics can make a positive contribution to teaching. Evaluation might include recording of work completed and stages reached by the children, diagnosis of possible reasons for children's difficulties and some form of assessment. Assessment need not involve standardised tests but can be devised to suit the teacher's own style of teaching. However, a good assessment procedure will enable teachers to diagnose where a problem lies. Diagnosis is not generally an easy task, for whereas assessment generally determines *what* a child doesn't know, diagnosis is more concerned with *why*. The following are some of the very general symptoms of low attainment in mathematics that may be noticed or 'diagnosed' in children. Suggestions are also given for appropriate remedial action.

Symptoms of low attainment in mathematics
1. Low attainment across a wide spectrum of subjects in school.
   Comment: After ensuring this is not due to a specific fear or general dislike of school, a generally more relaxed, structured and graded approach should be taken. Slower learning in itself need give no call for concern but it is common for children who fall behind to cease learning altogether and it is this situation that should not be allowed to develop.
2. Poor achievement apparent only in maths and not in other subjects together with a general dislike of mathematics.
   Comment: The cause may lie in a history of poor, unrewarding or sporadic teaching in mathematics, perhaps at another school or with another teacher. Alternatively, it may simply be that the child has a gap in his mathematical learning due to an extended illness. On the other hand, it may be that the teaching scheme itself is not sufficiently motivating for the child. More materials geared to the interests of the child should be tried and maths lessons generally made less stressful and demanding in terms of teacher expectations.

3. Particular difficulty in mathematics although the child has no particular dislike for this subject.
   Comment: Different approaches to teaching maths should be tried such as those suggested in Chapter 8, and a variety of remedial activities prepared. Try to create stronger motivation towards maths by means of activities such as those suggested in Chapter 3.

4. Very specific difficulty within a single mathematical topic.
   Comment: In this case a careful recording of just what a child has accomplished and what he or she should accomplish next may be sufficient to ascertain the exact nature of the problem. Some of the simple records suggested in the following sections may be helpful, although teachers should, where possible, devise records to suit their own circumstances. If a child encounters a number of specific difficulties in addition to general low attainment in several subjects, then it may be necessary to consider preparing an individual programme of more structured teaching steps such as the example given in Chapter 8.

Class records

Records used should be the result of a consideration of the needs of both individual children and the more general requirements of the school. They can be useful to both teachers and children when children are made aware that they *are* making progress, however slow that progress might be. Records should be used whenever there is a need for them. They should not be too detailed and should contain only information that can be acted upon. It is not always necessary to complete comprehensive records for all the children in the ordinary school class but extra consideration should certainly be given to those children whose achievements are falling behind the rest of the class. Some of the examples of record sheets given here have been adapted from those used in special schools where, however, the problem of completing records for a whole class is not so acute as in ordinary schools.

NUMBER

Recording pre-number activities

Although a very specific programme of pre-number activities in the infant school is neither practical nor desirable, it is nevertheless useful for the teacher to have some idea of the direction in which these activities should develop. Pre-number activities are usually

collected together under the headings of sorting (classifying), ordering (sequencing, seriating) and matching (correspondence).
Teaching can progress in stages as follows.

1. Sorting, ordering or matching objects without reference to any
   observable properties but merely according to children's own
   particular preference.
2. Using the perceptible characteristics of objects, such as colour,
   shape or texture, as criteria for sorting, ordering or matching.
3. Sorting, ordering and matching depending on the use or function of items rather than any perceptual properties. For example: (a) collecting together all the furniture belonging to a house;
   (b) arranging cards in order depicting different stages in making
   a cup of tea; (c) using sets of cards to match hats to the appropriate worker; and so on.
4. Sorting, ordering and matching different sized *collections* of objects as a preparation for work with number.

Detailed individual records in pre-number are not necessary for
each member of a large class. However, for particular children who
give cause for concern, a recording framework using the above stages
(see Figure 7.1) could indicate those pre-number activities the child
has successfully carried out.

Figure 7.1 *Recording pre-number activities*

INDIVIDUAL RECORD SHEET FOR PRE-NUMBER SKILLS				
Class: Year: Name:				
		Pre-number task		
Task	Teacher presents	Sorting	Ordering	Matching
1.	Items related by children's own criteria			
2.	Items related perceptually			
3.	Items related by use, convention, association, etc.			
4.	Different sized collections of objects			

Examples of the use of the chart

Task 1 might be to ask the child to *sort* out all the pictures he or she likes from those he or she doesn't like, or *match* each member of a set of horses to the members of a set of riders, where the allocation can be made arbitrarily.

Task 2 could involve *sorting* all the thin red triangles from the thin blue triangles, and all the thick red from the thick blue triangles. This is sorting perceptually according to *two* attributes or properties. Alternatively, the child could *order* a set of tins from the smallest to largest.

Task 3 might require the child to match a series of cards with pictures of various types of hats to each of a series of pictures of workers in different occupations (a baker's hat to a baker, a policeman's hat to a policeman, etc.).

Task 4 is a preparation for number work and should involve the children in *sorting, ordering* or *matching* small boxes of counters. For example, children could *sort* all the boxes containing five objects from those containing four or three objects or *order* a collection of strings of beads with different numbers of beads on each string.

Early progress with numbers

Children need to write and to recognise both aurally and visually the numerals (number symbols) from 0 to 9. They need also to count collections of objects and *count out* a given number of objects from a

Figure 7.2 *Recording stages in counting*

Class: Year: Name:	INDIVIDUAL CHECKLIST FOR NUMBERS 0 TO 100														
Task	Teacher presents	Learner's response	0	1	2	3	4	5	6	7	8	9	10	11-20	21-100
1.	Objects to count	Spoken numeral													
2.	Objects to count	Written numeral													
3.	Spoken numeral	Counts out objects													
4.	Written numeral	Counts out objects													
5.	Spoken numeral	Written numeral													
6.	Written numeral	Spoken numeral													

larger collection. In the early stages of learning number, teachers should record the following information for each child entering or leaving the reception class. Can the child:

1. Both say and write down the appropriate numeral for a given collection of objects?
2. Given either a spoken or written numeral, *count out* the appropriate number of objects?
3. Both read a written numeral and write down a spoken numeral?

The type of record sheet shown in Figure 7.2 has been used in Manchester special schools (Working Party of Manchester Teachers, 1979), and indicates this information individually for the numerals 0 to 9 and in groups for the numbers up to 100. A simple tick in the appropriate row or column will indicate a child's success in each activity.

Examples of the use of the chart
1. Although a slower learning child may count (orally) six objects given to him or her (Task 1) it does not necessarily follow that he or she can *count out* six counters from a tray before him or her (Task 4). These tasks are shown as distinct on the record sheet.
2. It may be that a child can name (orally) a written numeral (Task 6) and also count out that same number of objects (Task 3). However, he or she may be unable to put the two tasks together and count out the number of objects asked for in written symbolic form (Task 4). The record sheet will 'diagnose' these learning anomalies that often hinder children's early number learning.
3. By using the record sheet, a profile of a child's strengths and weaknesses in the six different tasks can be obtained and on the basis of this information, time can be spent on those numerals the child has yet to learn.

Teaching the number facts

For less able children a knowledge of number facts gives them much needed confidence in arithmetic and allows them to consider the meaning or application of a problem apart from its 'mechanical' aspect. It is important therefore to spend time in devising simple ways to make the learning of number facts (or number 'bonds') easier.

One effective way of teaching these facts is to divide an A4-sized sheet of paper into 36 squares and to write in each square all the addition facts with totals from 0 to 10 (see Figure 7.3).

0+1	0+2	0+3	0+4	0+5	0+6
0+7	0+8	0+9	1+1	1+2	1+3
1+4	1+5	1+6	1+7	1+8	1+9
2+1	2+2	2+3	2+4	2+5	2+6
2+7	2+8	3+1	3+2	3+3	3+4
3+5	3+6	3+7	4+1	4+2	4+3
4+4	4+5	4+6	5+1	5+2	5+3
5+4	5+5	6+1	6+2	6+3	6+4
7+1	7+2	7+3	8+1	8+2	9+1

1	2	3	4	5	6
7	8	9	2	3	4
5	6	7	8	9	10
3	4	5	6	7	8
9	10	4	5	6	7
8	9	10	5	6	7
8	9	10	6	7	8
9	10	7	8	9	10
8	9	10	9	10	10

Front of card *Reverse of card*

Figure 7.3 *Addition facts totalling up to 10*

Figure 7.4 is an example of a sheet containing the 36 subtraction facts that involve subtraction of a single digit (2 to 9) from a 2-digit number (11 to 18) to give a single digit answer. Similar sheets can be prepared for other number facts.

If the child colours in the appropriate number fact on the sheet as each fact is learned then these provide a useful record for both teacher and child. If answers are printed on the reverse side of each sheet immediately behind each question then the sheet can be cut up into individual rectangles and used in various ways as a personal learning aid. For example, various games testing knowledge of the small

Figure 7.4 *Subtraction facts totalling up to 10*

18–9	17–9	17–8	16–9	16–8	16–7
15–9	15–8	15–7	15–6	14–9	14–8
14–7	14–6	14–5	13–9	13–8	13–7
13–6	13–5	13–4	12–9	12–8	12–7
12–6	12–5	12–4	12–3	11–9	11–8
11–7	11–6	11–5	11–4	11–3	11–2

9	8	9	7	8	9
6	7	8	9	5	6
7	8	9	4	5	6
7	8	9	3	4	5
6	7	8	9	2	3
4	5	6	7	8	9

Front of card *Reverse of card*

'question and answer' cards can be invented by the teacher or children.

Diagnosing conceptual errors

Conceptual misunderstandings of the nature of a particular mathematical process are the most difficult to detect and remedy. Some teachers—for example, the Russian teacher V. D. Petrova (1981), see Chapter 8—have had much success in encouraging children to analyse their own errors in mathematics. However, while some children can be surprisingly frank and open about their shortcomings, care must be taken with any method of assessment in which the errors of one child are made known to the whole class. Some children, among them many slower learners, are either unable or unwilling to communicate their problems and difficulties and so a less direct approach must be made. In the case of arithmetic, careful observation of the child working through many examples is required if consistent errors are to be revealed, and this is not an easy task in a busy classroom. For example, if the given computation was one of addition, did the child recount the whole to reach the total or was counting-on employed? Was a knowledge of number facts used? Remedial strategies in response to the diagnosis should be decided upon at the time of observation. Answers to the following questions may need to be found if 'diagnosis' is to be effective.

- Does the child count aloud or use his or her fingers?
- Does the child always require apparatus in order to compute?
- Which apparatus does he or she prefer to use?
- Can the child write down an orally given computation?
- Does the child use the same method for orally given computations as for written ones?
- Are the child's errors simply those of poor knowledge of number facts?
- Does the child have difficulty with the physical manipulation of the structural apparatus he or she is using?
- Does the child make a systematic error or does the error vary according to the type of computation?

To attempt an answer to all these questions without some prepared format for recording responses is an extremely difficult task. The format in Figure 7.5 is an example of one that has been used in ordinary schools but teachers should aim to develop their own form of assessment. The recording format used should allow for the following information to be recorded.

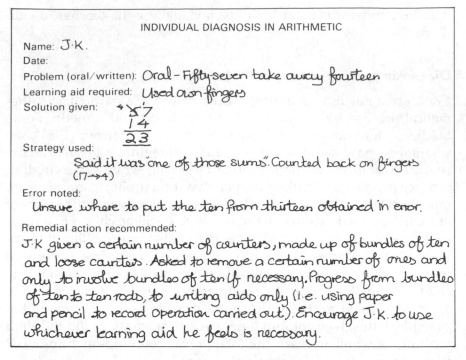

INDIVIDUAL DIAGNOSIS IN ARITHMETIC

Name: J·K·

Date:

Problem (oral/written): *Oral - Fifty-seven take away fourteen*

Learning aid required: *Used own fingers*

Solution given:

$$\begin{array}{r} {}^{4}\cancel{5}{}^{1}7 \\ 1\,4 \\ \hline 2\,3 \end{array}$$

Strategy used:
Said it was "one of those sums". Counted back on fingers (17→4)

Error noted:
Unsure where to put the ten from thirteen obtained in error.

Remedial action recommended:
J·K· given a certain number of counters, made up of bundles of ten and loose counters. Asked to remove a certain number of ones and only to involve bundles of ten if necessary. Progress from bundles of ten to ten rods, to writing aids only (i.e. using paper and pencil to record operation carried out). Encourage J·K· to use whichever learning aid he feels is necessary.

Figure 7.5 *Recording format for diagnosing errors in arithmetic*

1. Name of child and date.
2. The problem posed and whether given orally or in writing.
3. The answer given and whether orally or in writing.
4. The type of apparatus the child preferred and used.
5. The mathematical strategy used by the child.

Errors in computation

Errors in the computational aspects of arithmetic are a source of frustration and discouragement to children, and for children whose short-term memory is weak, a degree of rote learning of number facts may be necessary. This will allow time for reflection and understanding of the reasons for a particular method of computation.

It may be that a child is not able to give valid reasons for his or her (correct) method of calculation, but such a child should not be held back from further progress. Clarification and understanding may only come when a procedure has been used frequently or as part of a more advanced algorithm.

Below are some of the common causes of error in arithmetic.

1. Errors concerned with the exchange of tens, for example:

$$\text{i.} \quad \begin{array}{r} {}^1\cancel{3}{}^17 \\ -18 \\ \hline 09 \end{array} \quad \text{or} \quad \text{ii.} \quad \begin{array}{r} {}^1\cancel{3}{}^17 \\ -18 \\ \hline 30 \end{array}$$

In (i), the 1 *replaces* the 3 in the tens column. In (ii), a 1 is *added* to both the units and the tens columns.

2. Errors in dealing with the numeral zero, for example:

$$\begin{array}{r} 35 \\ +20 \\ \hline 56 \end{array} \quad \text{or} \quad \begin{array}{r} 60 \\ +18 \\ \hline 70 \end{array}$$

3. Adding a digit more than once, for example:
   $32 + 5 = 87$

4. Reversal of digits in the answer, for example:
   $63 + 21 = 48$

5. In subtraction, the most frequent error is to subtract the smaller digit from the larger, irrespective of the order of the sum, for example:
   $53 - 27 = 34$

6. Confusion with zero is common, for example:
   $50 - 26 = 30$
   $50 - 23 = 43$
   $72 - 40 = 30$

7. Confusion when subtracting a number from itself, for example:
   $5 - 5 = 1$

Teachers will know of many more but should be aware of those that are most likely to occur. The format in Figure 7.5 may be found useful in ascertaining the particular mistake a child is making. Alternatively, a useful diagnostic test for arithmetic errors is now available as a computer program from NFER (NFER, 1986). Suggestions are given in this chapter for teaching the number facts and in the following chapter for teaching the concept of 'place value'.

Recording progress in arithmetic

Formal arithmetic skills can be learnt successfully by all but the most severely handicapped children provided that plenty of practice is given and very gradual stages provided. However, children at any point of their school career may meet difficulty in understanding a concept or coping with a particular stage of arithmetic. Many mathematical assessment instruments are designed to help in this but these often require teachers to indicate which concepts a child has acquired. Concept acquisition is a complex process in young children and research has shown that the understanding of a concept is dependent to a considerable extent on the material used and the context in which that concept is met. Most concepts in arithmetic will be acquired as children carry out and practise the relevant algorithmic procedures and therefore it is essential that a careful check is kept on children who are showing early signs of confusion, since errors breed more errors.

It is important that a teacher should ascertain the arithmetical skills of new pupils entering a class and also—for those children experiencing difficulty—exactly where a pupil's difficulty lies so that suitable remedial practice can be given. It is also necessary to find out what a pupil *can* do so that teaching can build on the child's strengths and work can be given in areas in which the child is already confident. However, continuous recording of detailed stages is not a practical proposition for all children in a large class.

Figure 7.6 *Simple class checklist for arithmetic*

Class: Year:	CHECKLIST FOR BASIC ARITHMETIC								
Name	*Numbers 1 to 10*			*Numbers 0 to 100*					
	Numerals	+	−	Numerals	Place value	+	−	×	÷
						No ex. / Ex.	No ex. / Ex.	No ex. / Ex.	No ex. / Ex.

Ex. = exchange

Notes
1. *Numerals* An indication can be given in the first column whether all the numerals 1 to 10 can be recognised, written, understood and used (see Figure 7.2).
2. *Place value* The rectangles in this column can be progressively shaded in according to the children's understanding of the meaning and use of 'place value'.
3. *Exchange ('ex' in the checklist)* The most difficult formal computational step in arithmetic is that of exchange of tens, hundreds, etc. ('decomposition', for example, in subtraction). It is important to indicate when a child has successfully mastered this step in each of the four processes and this can be done by means of a tick in the appropriate column.
4. The checklist does not record which counting aids may have been used by children since this may vary from process to process and will alter rapidly as progress is made.

An extremely simple form of class record is given in Figure 7.6, on which the teacher can indicate the formal stages of written arithmetic attained by each child in the class. If dates are entered instead of ticks, the chart will show which children are taking an inordinate period of time over one particular stage so that extra help can be given.

Classroom resources for the remedial teaching of number

From the writer's experience of teaching in both ordinary and special schools, the following materials have been found extremely useful in assessing the more obvious sources of a child's difficulties in number. In each case a typical example of a use of the apparatus is given.

Resource apparatus for number assessment
1. Sets of plastic covered numerals 1 to 10 (raised lettering if possible). Also, numerals 1 to 20 and 1 to 100.
    Use Children can put several numerals chosen into the correct order.

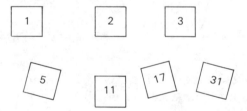

2. A number board with numbers 1 to 100 or 0 to 99 on which the small plastic tablets can be placed. A number strip 1 to 100 is also extremely useful.
    Use Observe how long it takes the child to place all the numerals on the board in the correct order and note any systematic errors.

1	2	3	4	5	6	7	8	9	10
11	12	13	14	15	16	17	18	19	20
21	22	23	24	25	26	27	28	29	30

1	2	3	4	5	6	7	8	9	10	11	12

3. A set of larger cards on which are written various numbers between 10 and 100.
   Use Structural apparatus such as bundles of ten, or ten rods and single units, can be placed on the cards to the value of that number. A selection of these cards can be left with the children who should try to put the appropriate value of structural apparatus on each. Checking of a large number of these cards on individual children's desks can then be conveniently carried out by the teacher. The reverse side of each card can be covered with acetate on which the children (using chinagraph pencils) may write the value of structural apparatus that has been left on the card by the teacher.

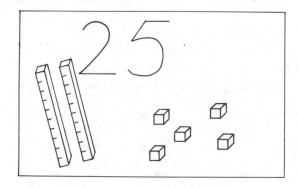

4. Large acetate covered cards divided into 'tens' and 'ones' columns and chinagraph pencils.
   Use For demonstration by the teacher of computational methods to individual children.

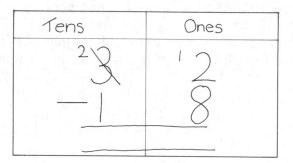

5. Sets of cards containing the numerals 0 to 9, the numerals 10 to 90 in multiples of 10, and the numerals 100 to 900 in multiples of 100—in the relative sizes shown (from Maria Montessori).

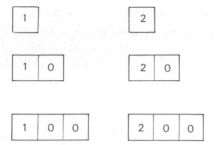

Use With just three of these cards, one selected from each set, any number up to 999 can be shown to be made up of hundreds, tens and units by placing one card in front of another as shown.

MEASURE

Planning a scheme of work

Children differ widely in their ability to both comprehend and to practise measurement, and careful organisation is required to ensure that all children have the opportunity to develop their skills in each aspect of measure (length, weight, etc.). Devising a scheme of work to cater for all levels of ability requires a considerable amount of apparatus if these different aspects are each to be adequately covered. Group work is therefore a popular mode of working to alleviate problems of shortage of apparatus and also to enable proper supervision of activities to take place.

A programme of work in measure is usually drawn up 'developmentally'. That is to say, at each stage of learning, all the topic areas (capacity, length, etc.) are dealt with. This is a convenient pedagogical framework but does not take into account the thematic aspect of certain topics. For example, if the class topic is 'time', then the children will be interested in *all* developmental stages in the measurement of time, whether by candle or by clock—particularly if different kinds of time measuring instruments are brought into the classroom. It may sometimes, therefore, be found more advantageous to work widely within each of these topic areas than to range across all topics at a single developmental stage. Measure can be usefully taught through sport, the class shop, children's personal sporting records and other achievements. Suitably interesting statistics can be obtained from books such as the *Guinness Book of Records*.

However, whichever scheme of work is adopted, attention should be given to the following developmental aspects that apply to each topic of measurement and with which children should be given ample experience.

1. The descriptive language of measure.
2. Pre-measure activities (such as sorting, ordering and matching).
3. Comparison of items: (a) 'directly' (for example, by putting two items side by side); and (b) 'indirectly' (for example, using an intermediary, such as a stick, to compare which of two objects is longer).
4. Conservation (for example, the children may believe that a lump of Plasticine broken into pieces will weigh more (or less) than the original piece).
5. Quantitative measure, using both 'non-standard' (for example, footprints, handspans, etc.) and 'standard' (for example, centimetres) measures.
6. Both the measuring aspect (for example, weighing a given object) and the measuring-out aspect (weighing out a stated quantity).
7. Use of calibrated instruments with which to measure (for example, dials and gauges).
8. Estimation of all measures (size, weight, etc.)
9. Knowledge of appropriate units and the relationship between them.
10. Written and oral problems requiring the application of measuring skills and knowledge of the relationship between units.
11. Measurement involving fractions and decimals.
12. Graphical representation of measurements.

Recording progress

Evaluation of measuring skills is a difficult task and there is a notable lack of suitably concise and practical records for use in the classroom. Checklists are often too general to be of use other than as a record of work taught, but if detailed objectives are specified for each topic of measurement, then the whole evaluation procedure may become too impractical to carry out for each member of a large class.

There is no entirely satisfactory answer to this problem of practical objectives and accurate records for measurement. However, if records are solely for use within the same school, then teachers can decide amongst themselves as to the relevance of any recording

MEASUREMENT—INFANT LEVEL

Name: _____
Class: _____
Year: _____

Language (underline the words understood)
Length: long, short, far, near, narrow, wide, tall, broad, high, low
Weight and size: heavy, light, great, tiny, huge, big, little, enormous
Capacity: large, small, full, empty, shallow, deep, half-full
Time: day, week, month, year, season, time, daily, soon, later
Other: some, more, less, all, none, much, enough, amount, plenty

Pre-measure activities
Length (e.g. ordering a collection of different lengths of rods):   _____ _____
Weight (e.g. sorting objects into heavy and light):   _____
Capacity (e.g. ordering containers of differing capacities):   _____

Qualitative comparison
Direct (items adjacent)
Length: which of two objects is longer?   _____
Weight: which of two objects is heavier?   _____
Capacity: which of two containers holds more?   _____
Time: which takes longer of two activities?   _____

Indirect (items separated)
Length: which of two objects is longer?   _____
Weight: which of two objects is heavier?   _____
Capacity: which of two containers holds more?   _____
Time: which takes longer of two contemporaneous activities?   _____

Conservation situations
Length: does the length of a line remain the same
   in different positions/configurations?   _____
Weight: does a ball of Plasticine weigh the same
   when broken into a number of pieces?   _____
Capacity: does the shape of a container alter
   the amount of liquid it can contain?   _____
Time: do children realize that different
   experiences can last the same time?   _____

Notes
Pre-measure activities: these involve sorting, ordering and matching. Only one typical example is given.
Qualitative comparison: Tick if children can successfully determine, for example, which of two adjacent objects is longer.
Indirect comparison: the children are required to use an intermediary object as a 'go-between'.
Conservation situations: indicate with a tick if the children affirm the statements when demonstrated in a practical situation.

Figure 7.7 *Recording progress in measurement—infant level*

MEASUREMENT—LOWER JUNIOR LEVEL

Name: _____

Class: _____

Year: _____

Non-standard units
Length: how long is an item (e.g. measured in hand-spans)? _____
Weight: how many beads—for example—does an item weigh? _____
Capacity: how much does a container hold (e.g. measured in cupfuls)? _____
Time: how long does an activity take (e.g. measured in pendulum swings)? _____

Practical skills
Measuring (standard units)
Length: finding the length of an item (in cm/m): _____
Weight: finding the weight of an item (in g/kg): _____
Capacity: finding the volume of a liquid (in litres): _____
Time: finding length of time an activity takes (hrs/mins): _____

Measuring out
Length: use of a centimetre rule and metre rule to measure out a stated length: _____
Weight: use of gramme and kilogramme weights to weigh out a stated quantity: _____
Capacity: pouring out a stated volume of liquid: _____
Time: timing an event in hours/minutes: _____

Relation between units
Length: number of (a) cm in 1 metre? _____ (b) metres in 1 km? _____
Weight: number of (a) gm in 1 kg? _____ (b) lbs in 1 kg? _____
Capacity: number of (a) ml in 1 litre? _____ (b) pints in 1 litre? _____
Time: number of (a) hrs in 1 day? _____ (b) days in 1 week? _____
(c) months in 1 year? _____ (d) mins in 1 hour? _____
(e) secs in 1 min? _____ (f) days in 1 month? _____

Using other instruments
Length: use of a tape measure to measure around objects: _____
Weight: (a) use of spring balance: _____ (b) reading circular dial scales: _____
Capacity: reading a graduated cylinder: _____
Time: telling the time using (a) conventional: _____
(b) digital: _____
(c) 24-hr clock: _____

Estimation
Length: (a) width of hand (in cm)? _____ (b) length of a room (in metres)? _____
(c) child's own height? _____
Weight: (a) the child's own weight? _____ (b) the weight of a child's shoe? _____
Capacity: (a) how much does a teaspoon hold? _____ (b) capacity of a kettle? _____
Time: (a) how long is the school break-time? _____
(b) how long until the end of school? _____

Figure 7.8 *Recording progress in measurement—lower junior level*

system adopted. Brief ticks can be entered on a relatively concise record sheet provided their significance is understood by all members of staff. For example, measuring the length of an object using either a centimetre or metre rule involves considerable practice and experience in different situations and to attempt to record each stage of learning in this skill would be tedious and impracticable.

In the following style of recording (see Figures 7.7 and 7.8), an activity that is central to the concept or skill under examination is described briefly in a short phrase whilst a tick against that item will indicate proficiency in all the general skills associated with that activity. For example, 'Finding the Length of an Item' (lower junior level chart) might require a child to measure ten items correctly with a small centimetre rule and ten longer lengths using a metre rule, although making no reference to fractions of units. The exact criteria used for entering a tick can be decided upon by the class teachers. Teachers can adapt such a form of record to their own particular circumstances and the information can then accompany children throughout the primary school. Those children behind in understanding or performance can then be identified at an early stage. The record sheet can also serve as a basis for a whole class record (omitting the language category from the infant level record).

SPATIAL CONCEPTS

Developing spatial work

A detailed developmental teaching scheme for spatial concepts is rarely found in the primary school. Many concepts such as those of laterality, body awareness, the topological notions of 'inside', 'next to', 'between', etc., and the positional terminology of 'in', 'on', 'up', 'round', etc., are better acquired in the natural environment of children's play or supervised PE. Physical activities play an important part in the development of children's understanding of personal body space. Physical exercise can also have a stimulating and therapeutic effect on children who may have an emotional blockage to learning. In addition, although many slower learning children are reluctant to participate in games and physical activities, these provide an opportunity for teachers to cultivate relationships with children in a setting other than the classroom.

Much spatial work can also be undertaken directly through art and craft lessons, as the following examples show.

1. Children can make patterns with triangles, squares, hexagons, etc., and all kinds of tessellations.

2. The five (platonic) regular solids can be made as Christmas decorations. Determining the relationship between the number of faces, edges and corners (faces + corners = edges + 2) can be made the basis of an interesting investigation.
3. Perspective, projections and the relationship of a shadow to its object can be studied from work in either art or science.
4. The most general properties of the circle can be understood from work in science or art.
5. The 'strong' properties of the triangle can be compared to the 'weaker' shape of the square in the construction of models.

Summary of spatial topics

For those who prefer a more systematic approach to teaching 'space', the following list summarises the main areas with which children should have experience (though not necessarily in the order listed).

1. *Awareness of body space and laterality* (naming parts of the body, the distinction between left and right, copying geometrical figures, the properties of mirrors, etc.).
2. *Language of spatial relations* (for example, the meaning of prepositions and adjectives such as *in, out, on, off, up, down, round, straight, curved, sharp*, etc.).
3. *The geometries of space* Topological awareness (*inside, outside, next to, touching, between*, etc.); projective geometry (recognition of perspective, distorted pictures, objects seen from unusual angles, objects seen from close up, shadows made by objects, etc.); Euclidean geometry (the 'usual' geometry of 2-D drawings).
4. *Solid shapes* Names of the solids (prism, sphere, etc.); properties (hollow, solid, regular, sharp); analysis of parts (faces, edges, corners, etc.).
5. *Plane shapes (surfaces)* Names of the shapes (triangle, circle, etc.); properties of parts (diagonals, bisectors, etc.); patterns (tiling/tessellation, rotational and line symmetry, reflection, etc.).
6. *Lines* Properties (points, neighbourhoods, closed/open curves, maze problems, etc.); axes and grids (systems of reference, making maps, constructing layouts, etc.); angles (acute, obtuse, right angles, sum of angles in figures, etc.).

Evaluation of spatial ability

A comprehensive evaluation of children's ability and understanding of spatial concepts is neither practical nor necessary in the classroom.

Nevertheless, teachers should be aware of those children who experience particular difficulty when dealing with spatial configurations. Several simple classroom procedures can be used to gain an initial assessment of spatial competence. For example, for young children, a well-known Piagetian test can be carried out using two identical 'model villages', with movable houses.

First, the child is asked to copy the teacher as she moves the model house on the village layout. Then the teacher's layout is turned through 180° (upside down from the child's viewpoint) and the child again is asked to place a house on his or her layout where the teacher has placed hers. This requires the children to adjust their perspective to the new 180° orientation of the model village. Full details of this task are given in Copeland (1979, Chapter 18).

As an alternative to this idea, a variety of spatial puzzles can be used to assess children's ability to deal with spatial configurations. An imaginative selection of such spatial tasks, games and activities is given in a small but useful book by Jean and Simone Sauvy (1974), working at the Decroly School near Paris. They trace the child's spatial development in the context of the mathematical notion of topology (the study of the general properties of space, such as nearness, connection and continuity). After using a number of such puzzles with children for some time, the teacher becomes familiar with the time taken to complete certain tasks and therefore learns what is an 'average' performance time for the task for a particular age level. The following are some of the spatial activities that have been constructed and used in the writer's classroom.

Activity 1
Building larger composite cubes from smaller (2 cm) cubes. Note the time taken for the child's *first* attempt.

Level 1 Use 8 cubes coloured red on three adjacent sides. The aim is to make a larger cube showing only red on the exterior.

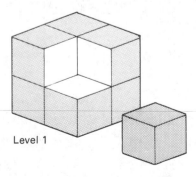

Level 1

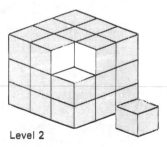

Level 2

Level 2 The same as Level 1 but using 27 cubes to make a 3 × 3 × 3 cube that, when assembled, shows red only on the exterior faces.

Extension Ask the children to *imagine*:

(a) How many of the small cubes making up the 3 × 3 × 3 cube have three coloured faces? (*Answer* 8.)
(b) How many have two coloured faces? (*Answer* 12.)
(c) How many have one coloured face? (*Answer* 6.)
(d) How many are uncoloured? (*Answer* 1.)

Level 3 As for Level 1 but the large composite 2 × 2 cube has six different coloured faces. (Each small cube has therefore three adjacent different coloured faces.)

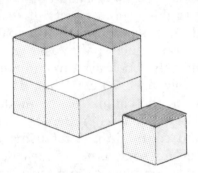

Extension (For more able children only!) As for Level 3 but each of the small cubes has *six* different coloured faces. The aim is to assemble the small cubes into a large cube with six different coloured faces (each face of a single colour). This is the classic 'six cubes to madness' puzzle—cube addicts be warned!

Activity 2
The teacher makes a three-dimensional shape from Multilink or other 3-D constructional cubes and the children are asked to make a copy of the same shape. The complexity of the shape can be made appropriate to the age of the children. A variation of the activity is to show the shape only briefly so that the children must copy from their visual memory of the shape.

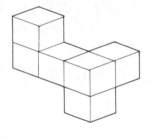

Activity 3—Kim's game
Show the children a tray full of objects. Unseen by the children, remove one of the objects, show them the tray again and ask them to say which one has been removed.

Activity 4

Ask the children to describe the inside of their house or a place they have visited. How would they escape from their house if both doors were stuck? What directions would the child give someone to reach his or her house—or the headteacher's study?

Activity 5

Various puzzles can be devised using a set of 'pentominoes'. Pentominoes are formed when five squares are joined together along their edges in different ways. These can be made with interlocking Multi-link or Osmiroid cubes, provided the unused locking protrusions are cut off the resultant pieces. The twelve possible pentominoes are shown in a 6 × 10 jigsaw. Other possible jigsaws are 5 × 12, 4 × 15 and 3 × 20. (See Chapter 4 for other activities with pentominoes.)

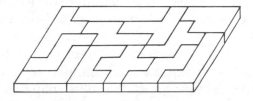

LOGIC

Logic and sets

The relationship between mathematics and logic has always been a controversial one amongst mathematicians. Piaget was perhaps reflecting the spirit of his time when he maintained that the construction of number went hand in hand with the development of logic (1952b). However, we are not concerned here with the purely formal relation between logic and the foundations of arithmetic. Children at primary schools are not ready to deal with logic presented formally or with mathematical proofs. General reasoning is best practised through purposeful activities such as those suggested in Chapter 4. Nevertheless, there are certain areas of logical thinking that can be usefully introduced to children of all abilities through other means than games and puzzles.

The formal system for dealing with the logical relationships between different classes of objects or events is that known as 'sets'. Although the relation of logic to arithmetic may be debatable, the power of sets to clarify logical thinking is unquestionable. Some of the properties of sets can be introduced through the 'pre-number' experiences of sorting, ordering and matching, but whilst these skills may be practised at an early age purely at a perceptual level, for the further development of sets, a system of ideas and a conventional terminology must be mastered.

Published introductions to number using set terminology are widely available to teachers who wish to use a 'sets' approach (for example, Williams and Shuard, 1976). However, a summary of the main concepts and terms is given below.

Summary of logical concepts and terms

1. *Logical classifications*

Logic begins at its simplest level with classifying items according to perceptual criteria such as shape, size, colour or texture. Later sorting can be on the basis of more 'conceptual' criteria such as 'all those children who have pets', etc., and diagrammatical representation can be made of these relationships (for example, Venn diagrams, Carroll diagrams, etc.).

More complex discriminations need to be made when considering two attributes at the same time (for example, separating items into the following four groups: all the big blue triangles, all the big red triangles, all the small red triangles, all the small blue triangles). Suitable pictures can be used to ask questions such as 'How many of the tall ladies have hats?', 'How many of the small men have sticks?'

2. *Logical relations ('is bigger than', 'is lighter than', etc.)*

These can initially be taught at a perceptual level, for example, ordering objects according to length, sequencing events (pictorially represented) according to their natural or logical order. Children can deal later with relations expressed by statements.

Relations can be *symmetrical*, for example, Steven *is the brother of* John and so John *is the brother of* Steven. Other relations may be *transitive*, for example, Jane *is bigger than* Sara, Sara *is bigger than* Gail. Therefore, Jane *is bigger than* Gail. These relations should not be taught formally but indirectly through other means such as questioning, for example, the teacher could ask the children (as a game), 'Who is your mother's brother's daughter?' or 'Who is your father's wife's son?'

3. *The terminology of sets*

This includes such terms as element, subset, union, intersection, disjoint, complement, universal set, null/empty set. The following example indicates, in ordinary language, one use of some of the more common terms but in no sense aims to be an explanation of the concepts involved:

The *universal* set is the set which contains all the possible *elements* which are under consideration. In this example it is a class of children. The set G of girls in the class is a *subset* of that universal set. The set B of boys in the class is another *subset* of that universal set. The set B of boys could also be described as the *complement* of G in the universal set (that is, those elements of the universal set which are *not* in G). The *union* of G and B is the set containing all the elements of both sets. (Elements which may be common to both sets are only counted once.) The *intersection* of G and B is the set containing those elements common to both sets. In this example there are, of course, no such elements: no children are both boys *and* girls, and so the set is empty. Such a set is called the *empty* (or *null*) set, since the sets B and G are *disjoint*.

4. *Logical terms*

The terms *and, or, not, if . . . then*, etc., have a well-defined usage and meaning in formal logic. However, at the primary school it is sufficient to ensure that children use these terms accurately and consistently. Practice should also be given in the proper use of the following words: *because, therefore, all, some, none, although, but, true, false*.

Below are the four 'logical connectives' used in formal logical reasoning together with their common and technical names.

Common term	Technical term	Logical sign (connective)
And	Conjunction	$\wedge$
Or	Disjunction	$\vee$
Not	Negation	—
If . . . then	Implication	$\rightarrow$

8

Teaching children with special needs

MEETING LEARNING NEEDS IN PROBLEM-SOLVING

One of the most important areas of mathematical and scientific thinking is that of problem-solving. The Cockcroft Report (DES, 1982, para. 368) suggests that one of the aims of mathematics teaching in the primary school must be to teach the ability to solve problems. In this section we will consider some of the learning characteristics of children's thinking when they are attempting to solve problems.

The Russian educationalist V. A. Krutetskii (1976) investigated some of the learning characteristics of both able and less able children solving mathematical word problems. Krutetskii found that less able children often failed to distinguish between essential and non-essential features in a question, and when they did attend to one relevant feature of a problem they tended to lose sight of another. They also found it hard to abstract themselves from the concrete context of a problem and did not appear to appreciate that mathematics often goes beyond sense experience. Links were made between different parts of a problem so slowly that the first part of the problem was often forgotten before the last was perceived and consequently explanations needed to be repeated many times.

The less able children tended to be inflexible in their approach, their work on a current problem being affected overmuch by the example they had just done and their habitual patterns of thinking were hard to change. They also found it hard to generalise from one or two examples, failing to realise that the method of solution to one problem would work for any number of similar problems.

Krutetskii also made interesting comparisons between less able children and able children, finding that differences between them were almost wholly of degree rather than in kind—that is, able children could attend to more than one feature at one time; they could curtail any links they made, enabling them to grasp the problem as a whole and had no difficulty in changing habits of thinking. In short, they tended to do things faster, more efficiently and more effectively than less able children. More radical differences seem to lie in qualities of personality and temperament. Gifted children had persistence and independence in working and a lack of those personality factors that adversely affect learning performance. This indicates again the importance of motivation in children's learning.

Many of the characteristics of the children in Krutetskii's study are similar to those found in children who experience difficulties of a more general nature in mathematics and so it will be useful to consider in more detail some of the aspects of learning involved in problem-solving.

Grasping the essentials of a problem

Children need to be taught how to look for the essential components of a problem. Significant words such as *more, less, added, taken, increased, decreased, altogether,* etc., should be pointed out and their meaning systematically explored.

The Russian teacher, V. D. Petrova (1981), studied children's strategies when solving word problems. In her teaching, she emphasised the correct reading of a problem and sections of the problem would be re-worded to determine the exact question being asked. She stressed the breakdown of a problem into its known and unknown parts and differentiated between closely similar concepts so that children at least understood what the problem was *not*.

Often problems can be too complex or too distant from a child's experience to be meaningful, except in the context of traditional puzzles such as, 'A man has to cross a river with a bag of corn, a hen and a fox...' As an example of the sort of confusion that can be caused by even the simplest of problems, consider the following question. Jane had four more marbles than Jason. Jason had sixteen altogether. How many marbles had Jane? A typical answer might be 'four'. In this case the child's thinking needs to be structured by the teacher. An example of the way this may be done is as follows.

Teacher Do we know how many Jason had?
Child Yes, sixteen.
Teacher Do we know how many Jane had?
Child No.
Teacher Who had more?
Child Jane had more.
Teacher So, Jane had more than sixteen. How many more than sixteen?
Child Four more.

Teacher So, four more than sixteen is...?
Child Twenty.
Teacher Good, so Jane had 20. Let's try another one...

This type of problem can be set out on the blackboard and systematically worked through to the benefit of all children in the class.

Abstracting from the concrete

Concepts need to be presented initially through concrete materials. However, if children are eventually to abstract their thinking from the concrete they need plenty of experience of meeting the same concept exemplified in different situations and with different materials.

Whilst there are advantages in initially teaching some concepts through a single medium or form of apparatus, if children are eventually to feel confident without apparatus they should at some stage be introduced to more than one type (see the example of teaching 'place value' in this chapter). One way in which this can be done is to ask children to solve simple number problems using many different forms of counting aids (beads, buttons, paper-clips, acorns, broken crayons, etc.). For example, a class of children can be asked to solve the following questions.

1. There are 23 children in Class 2. At break-time, 5 of the children stay in to help the teacher put up a frieze. How many children in Class 2 will go out to play?
2. There are 5 birds looking at 12 worms. How many creatures is that? Now each of the birds eats a worm. How many worms are left?

Children can use their different counting aids on the desk before them to work out the answer to the question. The apparatus can then be interchanged between the children. In this way children come to recognise that the role of the apparatus is only an aid to calculation and that the particular type of apparatus used is not important.

Attending to more than one variable at a time

Piaget has demonstrated on many occasions how young children tend to pay attention to only one aspect of a situation at one time. For example, when liquid is poured from one vessel into a taller, thinner vessel, children observe the higher level in the second vessel and believe there is now more liquid in the tall vessel, failing to take account of the narrower confines of the new vessel. Although this may be to a great extent a developmental feature of children's thinking, even at a mature age children have similar difficulty coping with two variables at a time (for example, length and breadth, time and distance or even the two spatial co-ordinates of graph paper).

Experience should be given with materials that demonstrate a change in only one variable at a time before children will be in a position to consider simultaneous change in two variables. For example, some 'logic' card games require players to look for both the same shape and the same colour. These can be adapted so that children need only consider the same colour (or same shape) at one time.

Remembering the constituent parts of a whole

Short-term memory can grossly affect the solving of word problems particularly when these are given orally. Children need to be given practice in repeating short oral problems, paying attention to both the information given and the problem posed. The information given can be reworded and recalled in a more succinct or colloquial form by the teacher.

Consider the following problem. 'A farmer had 17 sheep. He gave 5 to his brother and then another 6 to his young son.' This could be recalled by the teacher and abbreviated to: 'How many sheep had the farmer? (Answer, 17) 'How many did he give to his brother?' (Answer, 5) 'So he had 17, and he gave away 5, . . .' and so on.

Encourage the whole class to discuss such problems and allow the children to take as much time as they like, particularly for orally given problems. Initially children can use paper and pencil or even fingers if necessary. (Social pressures will eventually discourage the use of fingers.)

The following activities give practice in using the short-term memory.

1. Counting out aloud backwards (an aid to some computational problems).
2. Recalling a short series of digits read out by the teacher.
3. Including a problem as part of a story. Children can then be asked to recall the part of the story that includes the problem.
4. Writing down an orally given problem (mathematical dictation).
5. Verbalising a problem repeatedly even if it is a spatial problem. (Interestingly, studies have shown that children can remember a sequence of pictures as well as adults, though not it seems a sequence of words.)

Flexibility of approach

Less able children find it difficult when dealing with one kind of problem to switch to another kind. For example, after completing a series of subtraction computations a child will tend to treat each subsequent computation also as one of subtraction. This is one of the most difficult problems to overcome but teachers can accustom children to 'expect the unexpected' in a particular context by setting, for example, worksheets of addition problems that contain a single subtraction problem. Children can be told to look out for the 'odd one out'.

More generally, teachers can stimulate children to think imaginatively through suitable stories or by posing the sort of 'problems' suggested in Chapter 4, Imaginative thinking.

COMMON DISABILITIES AND THEIR REMEDIATION

The foregoing section has covered some of the common learning needs of less able children attempting to solve problems. In this section, more specific disabilities are noted, some of which may be due to inherent physiological handicaps. Some of the remedial activities suggested will doubtless be familiar to teachers in special schools who frequently encounter children with very marked perceptual, spatial and temporal disabilities.

More general suggestions for teaching children with emotional and learning problems are dealt with elsewhere (for example, Wolfendale and Bryans, 1979).

Short attention span, distractability and hyperactivity

Many less able children have a short attention span and consequently are easily distracted. The lesson style, format and topic should therefore be varied frequently. Children may then work hard for a short period knowing that they will soon be 'relieved' of their sustained effort and concentration.

Always ensure that work is appropriate to the child's level of understanding, possibly by having the children work in small groups. Carefully selected worksheets can be used for those children who find it difficult to begin a task. It is beneficial to both teacher and child if tension is relieved by allowing children to talk quietly about their work.

Perceptual disturbances

The inability to pick out the relevant information in a problem from the irrelevant has a literal counterpart in the physical act of perceiving. Some children may have great difficulty in seeing relevant detail in a complex context or background. The following are some activities that can be used to develop the important skill of perceiving.

1. Finding the hidden object in a 2-D configuration is a popular puzzle that specifically tests whether a child can pick out a simple figure from a complex background. The converse puzzle to this is to ask the children what they must add to a figure to create another given figure.
2. Guessing what an object is, from a photograph taken from a close-up or unfamiliar angle.
3. Guessing an object from its silhouette. (Children can make their own silhouette pictures).
4. Kim's game—a collection of different objects on a tray are shown to the children. One of the objects is then removed by the teacher, unseen by the class, and the tray is shown again to the class. Children are then asked to guess which object has been removed. A useful variation of this game is to walk around the classroom picking up the objects in full view of the children. As the children are later guessing which object has been removed, they can be encouraged to recall the sequence of movements made by the teacher when first collecting the objects. Noticeable improvements in the children's skill when playing this game were observed in the writer's own classes.
5. Picture completion exercises to find what obvious item is missing in a picture.
6. Encouraging children to notice and to recall objects and events seen out of school or, for example, on schools' television programmes.
7. Finding an identical pair of cards or spotting the difference between two cards, using commercially produced packs of cards.

Poor spatial awareness

The following activities may be found useful in developing spatial awareness.

1. Various outdoor games (rounders, netball, football, etc.) and structured gymnastic activities generally.
2. Making mazes from Plasticine or other materials.

3. Experience and play (if possible) with a full-length mirror.
4. Games involving the correct use of the left or right hand (for example, 'O'Grady says do this . . .').
5. Play with various commercially produced construction kits such as Lego, Meccano, Construct-o-straw, etc.

Young children who use either hand intermittently should be gently encouraged to use only one hand, the writing hand or the right hand preferably, particularly if this is already used for throwing or catching. However, the use of one particular hand should not be forced on an unwilling child. The dominant hand, leg and eye can be discovered by the following methods:

1. Observe the child writing (dominant hand).
2. Ask the child to catch a ball with one hand and throw it back again (dominant hand).
3. Ask the child to kick a ball (dominant leg).
4. Observe the child looking through a telescope (dominant eye).

Poor temporal awareness

Activities to aid an awareness of temporal sequence are as follows.

1. Learning number rhymes or any song.
2. Activities that teach ordinal number (see later in this chapter). For example, have the child count his or her own steps.
3. Recalling the events of the previous day or night.
4. Recalling a film seen or an eventful story told by the teacher.
5. Estimating when one minute has elapsed. (The teacher can hold a watch, tell the children when the time is starting and ask them to put up their hands when they think one minute has elapsed. Children improve remarkably at this game after only a small amount of practice.)

Poor hand–eye co-ordination

Activities to develop hand–eye co-ordination are as follows.
1. All drawing, tracing, colouring-in and cutting-out activities.
2. Drawing round and inside templates.
3. Drawing geometrical figures (circles, triangles, squares, etc.) and repetitive patterns.
4. Using an old typewriter or computer keyboard.
5. All ball rolling, throwing and catching activities.

6. Children acting as 'robots' and receiving instructions from the rest of the class as to which way to turn, etc.
7. Using any of the Logo microcomputer programs (see later in this chapter).
8. Model-making using commercial construction kits (Lego, Meccano, etc.) or using Multilink cubes.
9. Following around a maze (with finger or pencil and paper).
10. Various manipulation puzzles, ball-in-the-hole puzzles, classroom darts (tipped with rubber suckers), classroom skittles, guiding a ring over a bent wire that rings a bell if contact is accidentally made, etc.
11. Skipping in a rope held by the teacher or friends.
12. Doing all kinds of jigsaw puzzles including those that can be made in the classroom using Multilink or Osmiroid cubes (see Chapter 7, Spatial Concepts).

REMEDIAL TEACHING STRATEGIES

Teaching concepts

Concepts are not 'all or nothing' entities. They are sometimes merely a useful description of the ability to carry out a well-defined cognitive strategy or procedure in a number of different situations. However, a concept does not automatically transfer to all situations that exemplify that concept. There are few if any concepts children understand in *every* context and because the use of a concept is not evidenced on one occasion, this does not necessarily imply that the child lacks that concept. Children sometimes *forget* to use the understanding or skill they have acquired. (We as teachers often do the same thing when learning some entirely new skill—perhaps driving a car or using a micro-computer!)

The following points should be noted when teaching a difficult concept.

1. Begin with the familiar and specific before moving on to the more unfamiliar and general. (However, *always* to avoid general concepts and unfamiliar terminology defeats the aim of teaching maths and science.)
2. It is important to present the same concept through different concrete examples, *though not initially through different notations*.
3. Concepts should be presented one at a time. Children should not initially be expected to deal with more than one variable at a time.

4. Be prepared to present concepts through different sensory modes if necessary. For example, let the children count not only shells, sticks and beads but also rings of a bell, flashes of light, taps on the hand or even heartbeats (i.e. pulse rate).

Style of teaching

Teaching style is a most important factor when dealing with a class of children of heterogeneous abilities and it accounts for the very different responses different teachers obtain from the same class. Ultimately a class's response depends on the personality and attitude of the teacher but the following strategies have been found helpful in a wide variety of remedial teaching situations.

1. Involve the children in planning their own learning. In this way they learn how to learn!
2. Give plenty of praise and encouragement.
3. Give immediate feedback on the success (or otherwise) of any learning activity undertaken.
4. Offer help in completing work when necessary.
5. Allow opportunities to solve problems in familiar, non-stressful and informal situations.
6. Give children plenty of time to assimilate new ideas.
7. Use plenty of repetition although care should be taken not to sap confidence or inspire boredom.
8. Prepare the children gradually over a period of time for difficult concepts.
9. Give children lacking in confidence classroom responsiblities.
10. Encourage perseverance in a topic by changing the routine and mode of presentation (reading, writing, etc.).
11. Spend time alone with 'problem' children. For example, allow a child to help out with personal and classroom organisation at break-times. A 'problem' child motivated towards the teacher is no longer a problem!
12. Occasionally try a change of teacher with a particularly difficult child.

Teaching topics

The following teaching strategies are useful when teaching topics to a class of wide-ranging abilities.

1. Initiate and build topics around the child's interests.
2. Link topics to previous work or to first-hand experiences wherever possible.

3. Aim to make the topic as coherent, relevant and as meaningful as possible.
4. Don't stay on the topic for too long. A necessarily long topic should be divided into sub-topics.
5. Break a learning task into smaller parts whenever possible.
6. Ensure there is sufficient variety of presentation within a lesson (children should spend some time listening, writing, reading, drawing, etc.).

Behavioural teaching of maths and science

Behavioural teaching techniques have now been adopted almost universally for the teaching of mathematics to severely handicapped children and various forms of 'direct teaching' are carried out in most special schools. A structured approach via a series of objectives is usually recommended for slower learners and this style of teaching does have an important part to play (see the following section and Bibliography). However, two reasons have precluded a discussion here of the specialised techniques and merits of behavioural teaching.

The first is a practical one. Behavioural teaching requires a certain degree of training and preparation for its proper implementation and there are few classrooms where a teacher is able to devote the time and resources to planning and evaluating the strict procedures necessary to successfully carry out a behavioural programme of teaching.

The second is theoretical. This book is concerned with fostering and encouraging mathematical and scientific thinking, and while behavioural methods have proved to be effective in teaching skills to children of wide-ranging abilities, they are not, in the opinion of the writer, the most effective means of stimulating constructive or creative thinking in maths and science.

Rewarding of cognitive effort is often successful only in the short term and does not always carry over to other contexts in which no intrinsic reward is forthcoming. Efforts are sometimes made to link *extrinsic* rewards to *intrinsic* at a later stage of training. However, this is not a programme of work that can easily be undertaken in a typical primary school classroom without additional help and resources provided specifically to meet an individual need.

In contrast to this, teaching many aspects of maths through 'discovery' has become almost synonymous with enlightened teaching of primary school children. A major dilemma facing teachers is, therefore, which of these very different styles of teaching is most suitable for children with learning difficulties. It is the writer's belief that the answer to this will depend both on the teaching topic and the learning characteristics and personality of the child.

However, it is tentatively suggested that behavioural methods are most suitably used under the following conditions.

1. When no substantial meaningful link exists between the knowledge and skills already possessed by the learner and the new skill or concept to be learned.
2. When such a link exists but the learner is either unable or unwilling to recognise or appreciate it.
3. When the link with the material to be learned is in the nature of a 'mechanical' association that can be learned by rote methods.

If, therefore, the existing cognitive skills of the learner can be used at all, then they should be. This may not always be the easiest way to learn for many children, but when children use and build upon the cognitive strategies they already have then they are *learning to learn*. This ensures a firm basis of understanding for the future and for the hierarchical knowledge structures of mathematics and science.

PLANNING REMEDIAL TEACHING

The problem of teaching a large class of eager primary school children containing a small number of less motivated or less able pupils is a common if difficult one. There is no single or easy solution to this and whilst many excellent books deal with work suitable for a relatively small group of less able children (for example, Duncan, 1979) there is no single model of teaching that can be recommended for a large and heterogeneous class of children. Teachers must, therefore, adopt a style or approach best suited to their particular circumstances.

Keeping up with developments in mathematics and science teaching is not an easy task but ideas can be obtained from journals and summary research publications (for example, Dickson, Brown and Gibson, 1984).

Three different approaches to teaching are suggested in the following sections, each of which have been used in the classroom to cater for learning difficulties that ranged from remedial to more severe. The three examples deal with progressively more 'structured' teaching. Examples have been given of teaching strategies for specific topics, in the belief that teachers will prefer to generalise and to apply ideas for themselves from the particular examples given.

The first approach suggests a wealth and variety of activities and experiences in the selected topic area, the example being taken from a rather neglected aspect of early mathematics, that of ordinal number (the sequence aspect of number). Many less able children are notably weak in all areas of sequence, order and time, and these concepts play an important part in logical thinking and problem-solving. The activities are divided into those specifically involved with counting and those that emphasise order and sequence in a more general setting.

The second approach is more structured and specific, though central to the teaching of arithmetic. It deals with the systematic introduction of the concept of place value in the context of written computations. It attempts to develop progressively the concept through the use of various forms of structured apparatus commonly found in most classrooms.

The third approach is suitable for individual children who may be experiencing difficulties of a more severe kind and most closely resembles the behaviourally based 'teaching to objectives' or 'precision teaching' practised widely in special schools and elsewhere.

General activities for ordinal number

Whereas cardinal number is essentially a property of a group of objects in space, the notion of ordinal number is derived from a sequence of events in time (for example, sounds and actions). An ordinal number, therefore, describes the *position* of a single item in a collection rather than the size of that collection.

Much research has centred on the question of which aspect of number is first comprehended by the child (for example, Bryant, 1974). However, both cardinal and ordinal notions are implied in any counting situation, since counting imposes an order on a collection of objects and equates the ordinal property of each object counted with the cardinal property of that group so far ordered.

Activities leading to the notion of ordinal number

1. Have the child count ordinally (1st, 2nd, 3rd, etc.) the following sequence of events and actions: tapping of a ruler or percussion instrument; bouncing of a ball; number of skips with a skipping rope; banging two pebbles together; running around a circular course; chimes of a clock; steps taken by a child; and so on.
2. Have the child count ordinally the following objects: fingers of the hand from left to right (fingers always keep the same relative positions); books standing on a shelf; coats hanging on a line of pegs; milk bottles standing in a line; bottle tops or beads threaded on a string; a tower of Unifix counters; counting beads dropped into a tin held by the child (here the child is using his senses of sight, sound and touch).

3. Recording a sequence of events:

   (a) The child can draw a picture each day starting on Monday and writing '1st picture, '2nd picture', etc. Count the number of pictures at the end of the week.

   (b) Give the children a successive ordinal number as they arrive in the classroom in the morning or hold various races and assign ordinal positions to the children. Subsequently have the children arrange themselves into lines in that order.

   (c) Arrange the children in order of height, weight, size of family, etc., and record these results graphically.

4. Have the child *count out* using ordinal numbers, for example, ask the child to give you 'the 4th one', or 'do the 3rd one again'.

5. Have the child recall a sequence of events or experiences, for example, ask the child what he or she did when they got up in the morning, 'First I went to the bathroom . . .'

6. Have the child follow instructions, for example, 'The 1st thing you do is to trace over the picture', 'the 2nd thing you do is . . .'. Or, 'Put those toys in order. Which do you like 1st? Which do you like 2nd?'

7. Games of sequence—many games depend on an order of 'turns' and orderly progression (for example, Ludo, snakes and ladders, etc.). Scores can be recorded for other games by means of threading beads, building a Unifix tower or shading in squares on paper. Numeral cards can be arranged into their correct sequence and other commercial card games can be used.

8. Use ordinal language with the child, for example, 'Show me the next one . . . Which is the one before that? . . . You've drawn it three times . . . Now do it once more . . . Fold it four more times . . . How many times is that?' These sorts of situations lead naturally to a counting-on strategy in arithmetic ('6 and 2 more make?') as does the use of number ladders and number tracks, etc.

9. Worksheets—the figures below show three typical examples that can be duplicated:

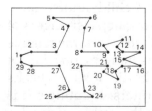

Colour the third star in green

Dot to dot   *Who will land second?*

Teaching the place value of number

This is one of the most important concepts in primary mathematics and the greatest source of errors made by children in arithmetic. 'Place value' is the convention whereby different values are given to a symbol depending on its position in a sequence of symbols. There are two component ideas in this as it applies to the decimal system.

1. A symbol's value depends on its position.
2. That value is either 1, 10, 100 etc.

Less able children have difficulty in making generalisations and therefore need wide experience of different kinds of apparatus relating to these concepts. These experiences may be considered in five stages as follows:

1. *Counting objects in tens* In order to gain experience of the second idea, children need to count large collections of objects into tens. These groups of ten are eventually to be treated as whole units and, therefore, gathering counters into boxes containing just ten is a useful first activity (see Figure 8.1a).

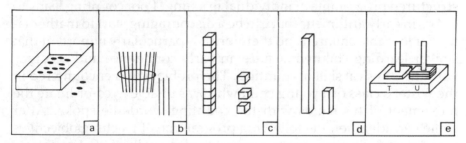

Figure 8.1

2. *Bundling sticks into tens* A natural second step is to bundle sticks into tens using elastic bands or alternatively to use ten interlocking cubes that can be pressed into a single length (see Figure 8.1b).
3. *Representing numbers with notched ten-rods* The 'temporary whole' ten-bundles of Step 2 are a natural preparation for the indivisible, though notched, ten-sticks of structural apparatus such as centicubes. These rods can conveniently be used to represent numbers displayed on a set of standard 15×11 cm white cards as indicated in Chapter 7 (see Figure 8.1c).
4. *Representing numbers with plain ten-rods* Experience with plain ten-rods such as Cuisenaire where 'tenness' is shown only by length (and sometimes colour) (see Figure 8.1d) is a natural step

towards the eventual disappearance of the intrinsic property of 'tenness' that characterises the apparatus of the next stage.
5. *Representing numbers on an abacus* When the number ten is represented by length, this tenness can still be recognised, however the counters are physically arranged. However, when children are solving computations without apparatus, there is no such cue—13 does not have the same value as 31. A suitable piece of apparatus to demonstrate this 'positional-value' property is the spike abacus where the same counter can represent either 1 or 10 (or 100, etc.) depending on which spike it is placed (see Figure 8.1e). If the step to using this apparatus is too great for a child then the abacus can be 'colour-cued' by painting the tens spike red and using only red counters on the tens spike.

Fears that children may come to rely overmuch on material aids are unnecessary. Once children acquire confidence in arithmetic they will be eager to do away with apparatus as soon as possible.

Teaching to objectives—counting

The topic of counting has been chosen as an example of a carefully structured programme of individual teaching. Poor counting leads to errors in early arithmetic that can be a discouraging start to mathematics for less able children and therefore it is particularly important that slower learning children acquire an early confidence and accuracy with the physical skill of counting. The problem was encountered in the writer's class of a young child who was unable to co-ordinate the movement of his hands with the counting words he spoke. After some consideration the following programme of teaching objectives was devised. The only apparatus required is a collection of counters.

Teaching objectives
1. The child should match each counter in the collection to another counter in a one-to-one correspondence.
2. The child should touch each counter of the collection in turn, once only, without omission.
3. The child should repeat the number names (1, 2, 3, etc.) in their correct sequence.
4. The child should say each number name to correspond with a sequence of his or her own hand motions (for example, while tapping a desk).
5. The child should say each of the number names to correspond with his or her touching of each of the counters in a collection in turn. This is the final objective.

Teaching to objective 1 The teacher presents in turn a series of red counters on to which the child places a blue counter. Next, the red counters are arranged in a line by the teacher. Again the child is asked to place a blue counter on each of the red counters. Finally, the red counters are scattered randomly and the child is again asked to place a blue counter on each, ensuring that none is omitted.

Teaching to objective 2 The child is simply asked to touch each counter in turn when: (a) the counters are placed in a row; (b) the counters in the row are moved closer together (thereby increasing the perceptual–motor skills necessary); (c) the counters are arranged in a circle, so the child must know when to stop counting; (d) the counters are scattered randomly.

Teaching to objective 3 The child must learn the conventional order of the number names by repeating slowly and clearly after the teacher. A set of large and colourful numeral cards will help to focus the child's attention on each number.

Teaching to objective 4 The child co-ordinates the sequence of number names learnt in objective 3 with a sequence of natural hand movements (for example, the child taps his or her desk while repeating the number sequence).

Teaching to objective 5 If the child has difficulty with this final co-ordination of the skills that have been carried out separately, this task can be broken down into still smaller steps as follows: (a) the child places a counter on one side when each number is called in sequence by the teacher); (b) conversely, the child repeats the sequence of number names (1, 2, 3, etc.) while the teacher moves the counters as each number is called; (c) finally, the child both says the numbers and touches or moves the counters—the normal counting process.

Although rhythmic counting is initially helpful to children, the rhythm needs to be broken occasionally to reinforce the essential correspondence between the number names and the counted items. Breaking the counting process down into a number of steps ensures that whenever a counting difficulty is encountered by a child the teacher is in a position to know exactly what sort of remedial activities will be most beneficial.

USING MICROCOMPUTERS

Commercial microcomputer programs now cover almost every

aspect of the primary school curriculum but due to the considerable number of them, those programs dealing with general mathematics will not be considered here. A note will be made only of the usefulness of some of these programs in stimulating the reasoning processes that form the main subject of this book.

Why use microcomputers?

Microcomputer programs are particularly suited to present a large number of examples of a concept in a very short time. From these examples children can form their own hypotheses and test them out within the program. This is a form of investigatory work that is not possible to conduct by other means. Their use as a database, handling and classifying large quantities of information supplied by the user, is also a valuable resource for science.

Recreational use of computers should be permitted if not positively encouraged since games and puzzles form a large proportion of home computer software and these can stimulate a good deal of discussion, involvement and motivation for children. Even such a simple device as filling the screen with the child's name can have a very stimulating effect on children who may have reservations about their ability to use a computer. As it has been so aptly expressed, children working with micros should be allowed to 'pick flowers along the way' (Fletcher, 1983, p.34).

Spatial work

Although microcomputers operate in only two dimensions they can play a valuable part in a child's spatial development. For example, many microcomputer programs require young children to be able to read and understand such terms as *left* and *right*, *up* and *down*, *inside* and *outside*, etc. Geometrical patterns are also a notable feature of many programs and some of the better known of these are listed under 'Spatial reasoning' in the list of Microcomputer programs.

A development from these pre-programmed patterns is the facility for children to create their own patterns through the use of the programming language Logo, first developed in America and enthusiastically promoted by Seymour Papert (1980). Geometrical figures can be created in two main ways. The most innovatory is that created by an electronic, turtle-shaped machine. The movements of this turtle can be controlled by a child typing onto a computer keyboard so that the turtle draws upon sheets of paper on the classroom floor.

A derivative method, known as turtle graphics, allows the movements of a point on a screen to be predetermined by writing simple programs incorporating such commands as TURN 60° LEFT, FORWARD 6, etc. These commands will create either simple or complicated designs according to the degree of complexity built up by programming with routines that can be compounded. The children's work with turtle graphics can be made as free or as structured as desired by the teacher (see Fletcher, 1983). Commercial introductory software to Logo is listed in Microcomputer programs.

Bigtrak
Another approach to spatial ideas is the use of a toy truck known as Bigtrak. This holds its own keyboard, which allows it to be programmed to negotiate an obstacle course by turning and by forward/backward movements. Logical route-planning, estimating, calculating distances and degree of turn are all involved in the simple programming of the machine. Motivation, discussion and general involvement of the children makes this a valuable introduction to more serious programming.

Drill and practice

We shall not refer to the multitude of drill and practice programs available. Some of these achieve admirably the limited purpose for which they were designed and such programs can be most useful in providing further extensive practice for low achieving children.

However, it is sometimes more useful to have the children type in a simple three- or four-line program designed by the teacher to generate a random selection of simple computations. Another three or four line program that can be copied and typed in by children from a small card prepared beforehand by the teacher will provide solutions for the child's work. This both frees the teacher from the need to supervise additional practice in basic skills and also gives individual children an opportunity to take some responsibility for their own progress in learning.

Microcomputers and the physically handicapped

The concept keyboard is an alternative computer keyboard that alleviates some of the manipulative problems associated with the traditional-sized keyboard. Many so-called 'robotic control techniques' are also available to assist the more severely physically handicapped child to use the computer as easily as the non-handicapped child. Examples of specialised modifications to the keyboard are pressing the keys with the feet, eyelid or even by a sudden breathing-in. Details of these innovations can be found in Stewart (1985).

References

Biggs, E. (1985) *Teaching Mathematics 7 to 13, Slow Learning and Able Pupils*. Windsor: NFER–Nelson.

Black, P. (1980) 'Why hasn't it worked?'. *Times Educational Supplement*, 3 October.

Bryant, P. (1974) *Perception and Understanding in Young Children, an Experimental Approach*. London: Methuen.

Buxton, L. (1981) *Do You Panic About Maths?* London: Heinemann.

Copeland, R. W. (1979) *How Children Learn Mathematics* (3rd edn). New York: Macmillan.

De Bono, E. (1972) *Children Solve Problems*. London: Allen Lane.

De Bono, E. (1976) *Teaching Thinking*. Temple Smith.

Denvir, B., Stolz, C. and Brown, M. (1982) *Low Attainers in Mathematics 5–16: Policies and Practices in Schools* (Schools Council Working Paper 72). London: Methuen Educational.

DES (1978) *Special Educational Needs* (the Warnock Report). London: HMSO.

DES (1979) *Mathematics 5 to 11* (HMI Series no. 9). London: HMSO.

DES (1982) *Mathematics Counts* (the Cockcroft Report). London: HMSO.

DES (1984) *Science in Primary Schools* (HMI Discussion Paper). London: HMSO.

DES (1985) *Mathematics from 5 to 16* (Curriculum Matters no. 3, p.27). London: HMSO.

Dickson, L., Brown M. and Gibson, D. (1984) *Children Learning Mathematics: a Teacher's Guide to Recent Research* (Low Attainers in Mathematics 5–16 Project, p.181). Eastbourne: Holt Educational.

Donaldson, M. (1978) *Children's Minds*. London: Fontana.

Duncan, A. (1979) *Teaching Mathematics to the Slow Learner*. London: Ward Lock Educational.

Elstgeest, J. (1985) 'Encounter, interaction, dialogue', in W. Harlen (ed.) *Primary Science: Taking the Plunge*. London: Heinemann Educational.

Fish, J. (1985) *Special Education: the Way Ahead* (Children with Special Needs Series). Milton Keynes: Open University Press.

Fletcher, T. J. (HMI) (1983) *Microcomputers and Mathematics in School* (p.34). London: HMSO.

Gardner, M . (1969) *Further Mathematical Diversions*. Harmondsworth: Penguin.

Harlen W., Darwin, A. and Murphy, M. (1977) *Match and Mismatch* (Schools Council Progress in Learning Science Project). Edinburgh: Oliver & Boyd.

Jenkins, E. W. (1987) 'Philosophical Flaws'. *Times Educational Supplement*, 2 January.

Keller, H. (1958) *The Story of My Life*. Sevenoaks: Hodder & Stoughton.

Krutetskii, V. A. (1976) *The Psychology of Mathematical Abilities in Schoolchildren*. University of Chicago.

Lovell, K. (1966) *The Growth of Basic Mathematical and Scientific Concepts in Children* (5th edn). University of London Press.

NFER (1986) *Diagnosis of Arithmetic Errors* (Computer Test). Windsor: NFER–Nelson.

Nuffield Maths Project (1972) *Checking Up II* (p.44). Edinburgh: W. & R. Chambers.

Papert, S. (1980) *Mindstorms: Children, Computers and Powerful Ideas*. Brighton: Harvester.

Petrova, V. D. (1981) in A. Floyd (ed) *Developing Mathematical Thinking*. London: Addison–Wesley.

Piaget, J. (1930) *The Child's Conception of Physical Causality* (p.36). London: Routledge & Kegan Paul.

Piaget, J. (1952a) *The Language and Thought of the Child*. London: Routledge & Kegan Paul.

Piaget, J. (1952b) *The Child's Conception of Number* (p.viii). London: Routledge & Kegan Paul.

Piaget, J. (1969) *The Psychology of the Child* (Chapter 3). London: Routledge & Kegan Paul.

Piaget, J. (1977) *The Moral Judgement of the Child*. Harmondsworth: Penguin. (First published by Routledge & Kegan Paul, London, 1932.)

Robbins, N. and Stenquist, G. (1967) *The Deaf–Blind Rubella Child* (Perkins Publications no. 25). Watertown, Mass: Perkins.

Sauvy, J. and S. (1974) *The Child's Discovery of Space* (Penguin Papers in Education). Harmondsworth: Penguin.

Somerset Education Authority (1981) *Ways and Means 2: Children with Learning Difficulties*. Globe Education.

Stewart, J. (ed) (1985) *Exploring Primary Science and Technology with Microcomputers*. Council for Educational Technology on behalf of the Microelectronics Education Programme.

Watts, M. (1982) 'Alternative Frameworks'. *Times Educational Supplement*, 19 March.

Williams, E. M. and Shuard, H. (1976) *Primary Mathematics Today*. London: Longman.

Wolfendale, S. (1987) *Primary Schools and Special Needs: Policy, Planning and Provision* (Special Needs in Ordinary Schools Series). London: Cassell.

Wolfendale, S. and Bryans, T. (1979) *Suggestions for Behaviour and Learning Management: A Handbook for Teachers*. Stafford: National Association for Remedial Education.

Womack, D. (1983a) 'Seeing the Light?' *Times Educational Supplement*, 8 April.

Womack, D. (1983b) *Maths on Television: Doing or Viewing?* London: Independent Broadcasting Authority.

Working Party of Manchester Teachers (1979) *Mathematics Guide for Children with Learning Difficulties*. Manchester: Manchester LEA document.

Select bibliography

CHAPTER 1

Brennan, W. K. (1979) *Curricular Needs of Slow Learners* (Schools Council Working Paper 63). London: Evans/Methuen Educational.
Croll, P. and Moses, D. (1985) *One in Five: the Assessment and Incidence of Special Educational Needs*. London: Routledge & Kegan Paul.

CHAPTER 2

Adams, P. (1970) *The First Book of Number Rhymes*. Westerham.
Adams, P. (1976) *Learning with Traditional Rhymes* (Ladybird Books series 702, books 1–6). Loughborough: Ladybird.
Deakin, M. (1972) *The Children on the Hill*. London: Andre Deutsch.
Green, R. T. and Laxon, V. J. (1978) *Entering the World of Number*. London: Thames & Hudson.
Holt, M. and Dienes, Z. (1973) *Let's Play Maths*. Harmondsworth: Penguin.
Hughes, E. R. with Rogers, J. (1979) *Conceptual Powers of Children: an Approach through Mathematics and Science* (Schools Council Research Studies). Basingstoke: Macmillan Education.
Piaget, J. (1969) *The Early Growth of Logic in the Child*. London: W. W. Norton & Co.
Singh, J. A. L. and Zingg, R. M. (1966) *Wolf Children and Feral Man*. Shoestring.
Werner, H. and Kaplan, B. (1963) *Symbol Formation*. London: J. Wiley & Sons.
Yardley, A. (1970) *Discovering the Physical World*. London: Evans.

CHAPTER 6

DES (1981) *APU: Assessing Scientific Development at Age 11 years*. London: HMSO.
DES (1985) *Science 5–16, a Statement of Policy*. London: HMSO.
DES (1986) *A Survey of Science in Special Education*. London: HMSO.
Driver, R. *et al*. (eds) (1985) *Children's Ideas in Science*. Milton Keynes: Open University Press.
Harlen, W. (1977) *Matching the Learning Environment to Children's Development: the Progress in Learning Science Project*. London: Schools Council.
Harlen, W. (1983) *Guides to Assessment in Education: Science*. London: Macmillan.

NFER (1980) *Record Keeping in the Primary School*. Windsor: NFER–Nelson.
Ward, A. (1981) 'Guidelines for early primary science education, five to ten years'. *School Science Review* 62, 220, pp.540–5.

CHAPTER 7

Bentley, C. and Malvern, D. (1983) *Guides to Assessment in Education: Mathematics*. London: Macmillan.
Feuerstein, R. (1979) *The Dynamic Assessment of Retarded Performers*. Baltimore: University Park Press.
Galton, M. and Croll, P. (1980) 'Pupil Progress in Basic Skills' in M. Galton and B. Simon (eds) *Progress and Performance in the Primary Classroom*. London: Routledge & Kegan Paul.
Gelman, R. and Starkey. P. (1983) *Addition and Subtraction Abilities of Normal and Retarded Children*.
Larcombe, T. (1985) *Mathematical Learning Difficulties in the Secondary School*. Milton Keynes: Open University Press.
Taylor, J. (1976) *The Foundation of Maths in the Infant School*.

Assessment Materials

Gillham, W. E. C. and Hesse, K. A. (1976) *Basic Number Screening Test*.
ILEA Schools' Psychological Service (1979) *Classroom Observation Procedure*. London: ILEA.
ILEA (1979) *Checkpoints Assessment Cards, Primary Pack, Lower Primary Pack* (materials available from Learning Materials Service, Highbury Station Road, London N1 1SB).
Scottish Primary Mathematics Group (1986) *Primary Maths Progress Tests, Stage 2, Pupil's Book, Teacher's Book*. London: Heinemann.
The Mathematical Association (1979) *Tests* (review of tests current in 1979).
Turnbull, J. (1985) *Maths Links* (record sheets and tests). NARE.
'Yardsticks' (1975) *Criterion-Referenced Tests in Mathematics*. Nelson.

CHAPTER 8

Bell, A. W., Costello, J. and Küchemann, D. (1983) 'Research on learning and teaching' (part A) in *Review of Research in Mathematical Education*. Windsor: NFER–Nelson.
Carpenter, T. P. *et al.* (eds) (1982) *Addition and Subtraction: a Cognitive Perspective*. Hillsdale, NJ: Lawrence Erlbaum.
Copeland, R. W. (1974) *Diagnostic and Learning Activities in Mathematics for Children*. New York: Macmillan.
Dickson, L., Brown, B. and Gibson, D. (1984) *Children Learning Mathematics, a Teacher's Guide to Recent Research connected with the Schools Council Project 'Low Attainers in Mathematics 5 to 16'*.

Gelman, R. and Gallistel, C. R. (1978) *The Child's Understanding of Number*. Cambridge, MA: Harvard University Press.
Ginnsburg, H. (1977) *Children's Arithmetic: the Learning Process*. New York: Van Nostrand.
Gulliford, R. (1985) *Teaching Children with Learning Difficulties*. Windsor: NFER–Nelson.
Hegarty, S. and Pocklington, K. (1981) *Educating Pupils with Special Needs in the Ordinary School*. Windsor: NFER–Nelson.
Hoyle, E. and Wilks, J. (1979) *Gifted Children and their Education*. London: HMSO.
Johnson, S. W. (1979) *Arithmetic and Learning Disabilities*.
Kaufman, N. L. and A. S. (1980) 'Creativity in Children with Minimal Brain Dysfunction'. *Journal of Creative Behaviour*, 14.1.
Rees, R. and Barr, G. (1984) *Diagnosis and Prescription, Some Common Maths Problems*. London: Harper & Row.
Reisman, F. K. (1972) *A Guide to the Diagnostic Teaching of Arithmetic*. Westerville, OH: C. E. Merrill.
Resnick, L. B. and Ford, W. W. (1981) *The Psychology of Mathematics for Instruction*. Hillsdale, NJ: Lawrence Erlbaum.
Straker, A. (1983) *Maths for Gifted Pupils*. York: Longman.

Diagnostic evaluation and structured programmes for the teaching of mathematics

Adams, S., Ellis, C. L. and Beeson, B. F. (1977) *Teaching Mathematics with Emphasis on the Diagnostic Approach*. London: Harper & Row.
Ainscow, M. and Tweddle, D. (1979) *Preventing Classroom Failure: an Objective Approach*. Chichester: Wiley & Son.
Ainscow, M. and Tweddle, D. (1984) *Early Learning Skills Analysis*. Chichester: Wiley & Sons.
Distar Arithmetic (1976). Engelmann & Carnine.
Goodstein, H. A. (1979) 'Assessment and programming in mathematics for the handicapped', in E. L. Meyen (ed).
Instructional Planning for Exceptional Children. Love Publications.
Science Research Associates (1975) *Criterion Referenced Measurement Programme: Mathematics*.
Seville, E. W. (1952) *Easy Steps in Arithmetic* (series). Welwyn: James Nisbet & Co.

Microcomputers

Hoare, G. and Powell, M. (1985) *Mathematics with a Microcomputer*. London: Ward Lock.
Hogg, B. *Microcomputers and Special Educational Needs* (Developing Horizons in Special Education Series, 5). NCSE.
Noss, R. *et al.* (1985) *Microworlds: Adventures with LOGO*. London: Hutchinson Educational.

Obrist, A. J. (1983) *The Microcomputer and the Primary School*. Sevenoaks: Hodder & Stoughton.

Smith, R. S. and Watts, L. (1983) *Usborne Guide to Better Basic*. London: Usborne Publications. (A beginner's guide to writing programs.)

Stewart, J. (ed) (1985) *Exploring Primary Science and Technology with Micro-computers*. Council for Educational Technology on behalf of the Microelectronics Education Programme.

Science and maths for physically handicapped children

Barrington, D. (1987) 'Building bridges'. *Times Educational Supplement*, 2 January.

Christchurch College (1982–3) *Chess for the Physically Handicapped*. SEFT.

Goldberg, E. P. (1979) *Special Technology for Special Children*. Baltimore: University Park Press.

Hodgeson, A. (1984) 'Integrating physically handicapped children in the ordinary school'. *Special Education: Forward Trends*, vol. 11, no. 1.

Jones, A. V. 'Science for the physically handicapped'. *Special Education: Forward Trends*, vol. 7, no. 3.

Jones, A. V. (1983) *Science for Handicapped Children* (Human Horizon series). London: Souvenir Press.

Leach, G. (1982) 'Making science more accessible'. *Special Education: Forward Trends*.

RADAR, *Educational Implications of Disability, a Guide for Teachers*.

Research Centre for the Education of the Visually Handicapped (1982–5) *Guide for Teachers of Primary Maths to Visually Handicapped* (Research Programme in the Department of Special Education). University of Birmingham.

Scientific Activities for Visually Impaired Pupils Project (SAVI), University of California.

Resources for primary maths and science

THINKING MATHEMATICALLY (chapter 3)

Bolt, B. (1982) *A Resource Book for Teachers: Mathematical Activities*. Cambridge: Cambridge University Press.

Catherall, E. (1982) *Investigating – Numbers*. Hove: Wayland.

Gibbs, W. *Pebble Math Activities*. Hove: Jonathan Press.

Holt, M. (1973) *Fun with Numbers*. London: Piccolo.

ILEA Learning Resources Branch (1985) *Count Me In* (23 number-game cards, pack of cards numbered 1–100, blank cards, teacher's book. Designed for children with special educational needs.) London: ILEA.

Kirkby, D. R. (1983) various 'Maths Games in the Classroom' booklets. For full list, send to Eigen Publications, Maths Education Centre, Sheffield City Polytechnic, 25 Browngrove Road, Sheffield.

Kohl, H. (1978) *Writing, Maths and Games in the Open Classroom*. London: Methuen.

Shell Centre for Mathematical Education, University of Nottingham (1984). *Problems with Patterns and Numbers*. Joint Matriculation Board, Manchester.

Williams, M. and Somerwill, H. (1982) *40 Maths Games to Make and Play*. London: Macmillan.

Calculators

Bailey, A. and Haigh, G. (1985) *Electronic Calculators*. London: Longman.

Nuffield Foundation, Nuffield 5–11 'Electronic Calculators' Teachers' Handbook.

Open University 'Calculators in Primary Schools' (course booklet).

Shell Centre, Pack of decimals/fractions/calculators Worksheets. Shell Centre for Mathematical Education, University of Nottingham.

Walsall LEA (1983) *Walsall Primary Schools Calculator Guide*.

Books for children and teachers

Ball, J. (1983–1985) *Johnny Ball's Maths Games* (radio series teacher's notes). London: BBC Publications.

BBC and ITV (1988) *Radio and Television Programmes for Schools*.

Diagram Group (1984) *Facts and Figures of Number*. London: Longman.

Emmet, E. (1976) *The Puffin Book of Brain Teasers*. Harmondsworth: Penguin.
Marsh, L. (1980) *Guinness Mathematics Book*. Enfield: Guinness Superlatives.

Journals containing ideas for primary maths teaching

Mathematics in School (published by the Mathematical Association). Journal issues with ideas for maths of all kinds, including addresses: *Maths in School*, vol. 15, no. 1 (January 1986), *Maths in School*, vol. 16, no. 1 (January 1987).
Mathematics Round the Country (a magazine for primary teachers published by the Mathematics Association).
Mathematics Teaching (the Association of Teachers of Mathematics).

DEVELOPING REASONING (chapter 4)

Ball, J. (1982) *Johnny Ball's Think Box*. Harmondsworth: Penguin.
Bolt, B. (1985) *The Amazing Mathematical Amusement Arcade*. Cambridge University Press.
Bolt, B. (1985) *More Mathematical Activities*. Cambridge University Press.
Diagram Group (1982) *Baffle Puzzles* (series). Sphere Books. (Includes number puzzles, logic puzzles, picture puzzles, practical puzzles, mazes and labyrinths, etc.)
Fenby, T. P. (1982) *The Piper of Dreams*. Sevenoaks: Hodder & Stoughton.
Gardiner, A. (1986) *Mathematical Puzzling*. Oxford University Press.
Gardner, M. (1966) *More Mathematical Puzzles and Diversions*. Harmondsworth: Penguin.
Gardner, M. (1969) *Further Mathematical Diversions*. Harmondsworth: Penguin.
Hatch, G. (1984) *Puzzle Cards, Bounce to It, Jump to It*, etc. Copies from Department of Sciences Education, Manchester Polytechnic, Wilmslow Road, Manchester.
Holt, M. (1980) *Puma Puzzles*. London: Collins.
Holt, M. (1981) *Answer Me This*. London: Piccolo.
Holt, M. and Ridout, R. (1976) *The Big Book of Puzzles*. Harmondsworth: Penguin.
Howarth, A., Love, E. and McIntosh, A. (1982) *Points of Departure 1 & 2*. Association of Teachers of Mathematics.
Torrance, E. P. (1970) *Encouraging Creativity in the Classroom*. W. C. Brown.
Ward, A. (1975) *Simple Science Puzzles*. London: Batsford.
Ward, A. (1977) *Science Tricks and Puzzles*. London: Batsford.
Williams, K. (1980) *Masquerade*. Sevenoaks: Hodder & Stoughton.

Logical Thinker, a magazine suitable for more able and gifted children, published by Keesing International.

STIMULATING SCIENTIFIC THINKING (chapter 5)

Association for Science Education (1985) *Choosing Published Primary Science Materials for Use in the Classroom*. Hatfield.

Bainbridge, J. W., Stockdale R. W. and Wastnedge, E. R. (1970) *Junior Science Sourcebook*. London: Collins.

Brown, D. (1985) *Goldmine: Resources for Teachers*. Epistemology, 62 Newlands Road, Worthing, Sussex.

Hodgson, B. and Scanlon, E. (eds) (1985) *Approaching Primary Science*. London: Harper & Row.

Lancashire County Council (1981). *Science in the Primary School*.

Lloyd-Jones, R. (1985) *How to Produce Better Worksheets*. London: Hutchinson.

Showell, R. (1979) *Teaching Science to Infants*. London: Ward Lock.

Showell, R. (1983) *Practical Primary Science, a Source Book for Teachers*. London: Ward Lock.

Stein, S. (1982) *The Science Book*. London: Heinemann.

The Engineering Council (1985) *Problem-Solving: Science and Technology in Primary Schools*. SCSST, December.

UNESCO (1973) *New Unesco Source Book for Science Teachers*. London: Heinemann.

UNESCO (1980) *Unesco Handbook for Science Teachers*. London: Heinemann.

Ward, A. (1983) *A Source Book for Science Education*. Sevenoaks: Hodder & Stoughton.

Ward, A. (1983) *Tricks with Science, Words and Numbers*. London: Batsford.

Articles

Squires, A. (1980) 'What is science for primary school children?'. *Education 3–13*, **8**, 1.

Ward, A. (1981) 'Thoughts on the style of primary science'. *School Science Review*, **61**, 216.

Ward, A. (1981) 'Guidelines for early primary science education'. *School Science Review*, **62**, 220.

Womack, D. (1986) 'On Safari in Your Own Backyard'. *Guardian*, 12 August.

Science schemes

Science 5–13 Project (1972–5) London: Schools Council, 26 source books. Also, *With Objectives in Mind, Early Experiences*. London: Macdonald.

Teaching Primary Science (1975–8). London: Macdonald (a Chelsea College/ Nuffield Project).

Look! Primary Science Project (1981) Gilbert C. and Matthews, P., packs of workcards (pack A, 7–9 years, pack B, 9–11 years and teacher's guide). Wokingham; Addison–Wesley.

Learning Through Science Project (1980–2) London: Schools Council, 12 units, including *Formulating a School Policy, Science Resources*, etc.

Exploring Primary Science and Technology (1982) Brown, C. and Young, B. 4 units including pupils' cards, teacher's cards, *What to Explore* cards, record sheets, teacher's guide. Cambridge University Press.

Journals with ideas for primary science teaching

School Science Review.
Education 3–13.
Primary Science Newsletter.
Primary Science Review.

Examples of books for children suitable as 'science motivators'

Asking questions
   The How and Why Wonder Book of Science Experiments (series) (1964) Keen, M. L. London: Transworld.
   The Little Prince Antoine de Saint Exupery, Puma.
   1000 Questions and Answers (1974) Hardy, E. (ed.). London: Octopus.
Discussing popular science mysteries
   The World of the Unknown (series). London: Usborne.
   Arthur C. Clarke's Mysterious World (1982) Welfare, S. and Fairley, J. London: Fontana.
Performing unusual experiments
   Experiments with Everyday Objects (1976) Goldstein-Jackson, K. London: Souvenir.
   Science Can Be Fun (1982) Wicks, K. London: Macmillan.
Investigating the environment
   Looking at Science 2: The Natural World (1984) Fielding, D. Oxford: Basil Blackwell.
   Nature Themes, Education in Action (1975) Proctor, E. London: Evans.
   Children as Naturalists (1965) Hutchinson, M. M. London: Allen & Unwin.
   Unlocking Nature's Secrets (1984) Bright, M. London: BBC (Ariel Books).
Making working models
   Simple Science Experiments (1964) James, A. Huddersfield: Schofield & Sims.
   Make It with Hart (1979) Hart, A. London: G. Wizzard/André Deutsch.
Studying interesting objects
   How It Works. Loughborough: Ladybird.
   Inventions and Discoveries (1978) Williams, B. London: Franklin Watts.
Making connections
   Think of a Number (1979) Ball, J. London: BBC.
Learning amazing facts and records
   The Story of Mathematics (1968) Rogers, J. T. Leicester: Brockhampton Press.
   Guinness Book of Records (current year) London: Guinness Superlatives.
   Famous Names in Science (1979) Clark, P. Hove: Wayland Publishers.

General science series for children

These include: Macdonald Starters, Dolphin Science Books, Science Book of Fun (Usborne), Pocket Scientist, etc.

Science organisations

Association for Science Education (ASE).

Science and Technology Regional Organisations (SATRO) – 24 local resource centres for science teaching.

The Molecule Club – travelling 'science' plays for children run by Sir Bernard and Lady Miles. Details from Mermaid Theatre, Puddle Dock, London EC4V 3DB.

Microcomputer programs

See your local SEMERC (Special Education Microelectronic Resources Centre) for up-to-date details of programs currently available.

Programs suitable for use with children at all levels of ability. The key to publishers is at the end of the list.

CHAPTER 3

Mathematical Investigations in the Classroom (10 programs) (CM)
Mathematical Games and Activities in the Classroom 1 & 2 (CM)
Number Puzzles (ESM)
Jars (A)
Planet Measuron (EB)

Packages

Maths with a Story 1 & 2 (BBC publication from the radio series)
Basic Maths (ITV television series)
Micro-Primer series (MEP)
Problem Solving (25 programs) (WIL)
Maths with a Micro (H)

In-service packs

Some More Lessons in Mathematics with a Microcomputer (ATM)
Micros in the Mathematics Classroom (2nd edn) (L) (Shell/ITMA)
Primary Maths and Micros (MEP) National Project Team

CHAPTER 4

Investigations

'L' a Mathemagical Adventure (ATM)
Ergo (part of package 3)
Aspir (part of package 4)
Snook (part of package 4)

Logical thinking

Sheepdog (L)
Farmer (part of package 3)
Hunt the Thimble (G)
Infant Farmer (CUP)

Spatial reasoning

Pirates (part of package 5)
Tessellations (CUP)
Geometric Design (WIL)
Match Up (ED)

Games of strategy

Othello (CA)
Educational Games (WIL)

Puzzle solving

Picture Puzzles (MM)
Sliding Block/Jigsaw Puzzle (EBS)
Logic Puzzles (ESC)
Droom (R)

Imaginative thinking

Dragon World (4)
Granny's Garden (4)

CHAPTER 5

Database programs

Animal (T)
Tree of Knowledge (A)
Think (L)
Seek (L)
Matchbox (R) (with concept
keyboard)
Lists (part of Blue File – free from
SEMERC)
Animal/Vegetable/Mineral (B)

Science programs

Suburban Fox (G)
Pipistrelle (G)
Growing a Plant (H)
Survival (SCM)
Constellation
Locks (M)
Timer (ESM) (includes 10 pupil
workcards)
Meter (ESM) (includes 10 pupil
workcards)

CHAPTER 8

Logo programs

Logo Challenge (AW) (with
teacher's guide)
Dart (AU)
Turtle Graphics (A)
Crash (pre-Logo) (part of package 3)
Walk (pre-Logo) (part of package 3)

Special needs

Blue File – Package (free from
SEMERC)

Key to microcomputer software publishers

4	4mation Educational Resources
A	Acornsoft/ESM
ATM	Association for Teachers of Mathematics
AU	AUCBE/ESM
AW	Addison–Wesley
B	Bourne Educational Software
CA	Cambridge Project
CM	Capital Media
CUP	Cambridge University Press
EB	Encyclopaedia Britannica International
EBS	Ega Beva Software/ESM
ED	ED Soft
ESC	Educational Software Company
ESM	ESM
G	Ginn
H	Heinemann
L	Longman
M	Mape
MCM	Macmillan
MEP	Microelectronics Education Programme
MM	Micro Maths
R	Resource
T	Tecmedia
WIL	Alan Wiltshire

Name Index

Subject Index